30 Ways to Shine as a New Employee

A Guide to Success in the Workplace

Written by
Denise Bissonnette

Illustrations by
John Howarth

A Milt Wright & Associates, Inc. Publication
www.miltwright.com

About the Illustrator

The cover and illustrations gracing the pages of this guide are the contributions of Southern California's Freelance Artist, John Howarth. His talents have been commissioned by a wide range of customers for a variety of purposes including personal portraits, murals, posters and storyboards for film and video. In addition to his work as an illustrator, John shares his passion for art as a teacher at the Art Center College of Design in Pasadena and at Pasadena High School. John teamed up with Denise Bissonnette in her previous publication, Cultivating True Livelihood: Work in the 21st Century. For more information on the services of this gifted illustrator, you may call (818) 708-3493 or write to 6820 Baird Ave., Studio B, Reseda, CA. 91335.

Copyright 1999 Milt Wright & Associates, Inc.
Chatsworth, CA
(800) 626-3939

ISBN # 0942071-36-0

Printed in the United States of America

Dedication

I lovingly dedicate this work to two special friends:

*Joan Fountain, whose short-lived life is a constant reminder
to not miss a single opportunity to shine; and*

*Renee DeMar, whose friendship is
an ever-present sun in my life!*

Acknowledgements

The book you are holding is a testament to the power and magic of true teamwork. To my fellow contributors I offer heartfelt appreciation: **Anita Lee Wright** - whose discerning eye as an editor and magic hand as a lay-out artist touched every page; and **John Howarth** - an illustrator of extraordinary talent whose love for his own craft is reflected in the beauty and vibrancy he brought to this book. Thank you both for making this work not only more readable, but beautiful as well!

Table of Contents

Habits for Success

Gifts of Perspective and Choice

Take the Bitter with the Sweet

Making the Job Work for You

"I always knew that one day
I would take this road
but yesterday
I did not know today
would be the day."

- Nagaruna

Purpose of this Guide

Congratulations! If you are holding this book, I know that one of two things is happening - you have either just become a new employee or you are going to become a new employee soon! Either way, you are about to set out on a new journey and the purpose of this guide is to help you make it a great one!

No matter what job or position you are in or what company or organization you are working for, you will find ideas on each page of this guide to help you bring joy and success to the work you do. I don't know who I am more excited for - you, or the employer who is lucky enough to have you!

Today you are born to a fresh, new glorious day that has never been lived before and will never be lived again!

This is a do-it-yourself guide - a practical collection of ideas, tips and suggestions that will enhance your work life. The aim of this guide is to lead you in hundreds of little ways to grow in confidence and productivity, adding value to your employer, even as a brand new employee!   By following the suggestions laid out in this guide, you will come to see and appreciate the immense power available to you through the choices you make and the actions you take each and every day! By employing the incredible power of your spirit, your skills, and your own personal style, you are about to enjoy success not only in your work life, but in the rest of your life as well.

Organization of the Guide

The Thirty Skills

"Every small, positive change we can make in ourselves repays us in confidence in the future."

- Alice Walker

This guide is meant to be read one skill at a time, taking one skill per day or as you choose. Some of the skills are more detailed and will take longer than a day. Move through this guide at your own pace. As the Chinese saying goes, "Do not be afraid of going slowly. Be afraid of standing still."

This is your personal guide to read, reread, underline, highlight, be inspired by and share with co-workers, employees, the boss, family and friends. Each of the 30 skills is connected to the one preceding it and leads up to the following one, yet each skill stands independently, to be turned to as a reference and resource. The ideas in this guide can be turned to again and again, used in fresh and creative ways for years to come in every job you ever have.

The "Challenge of the Day"

Each skill also contains a "Challenge of the Day" which is a set of specific tasks or assignments for you to complete that allows you to put the tips or suggestions into immediate practice. These tasks and assignments are simple and straight-forward and almost always require interaction between you and other people in the workplace or your observations of those around you.

Do not miss the daily opportunity to stretch yourself in a brand new way.

Daily Notes

At the back of the guide you will find a section called Daily Notes. This section is to be used as your personal journal for taking notes, making observations, writing questions, and responding to many of the daily assignments with each of the 30 skills.

Food for the Soul

As human beings we live very intricate and multi-faceted lives. It is said that we not only have work lives, but we juggle at the same time a family life, a social life, a spiritual life and a physical life! (And we wonder why we are so tired!) I prefer to think of us as having *one life* - one integrated life that contains all those various aspects, not unlike branches of one tree. Naturally, the health and vitality in one area of our life affects all the others. Therefore, the daily assignments are not limited to the workplace. From time to time, you will be asked to engage in activities that extend into your family, social and personal life. It is important to pay attention to all areas of your life during this time of transition. In this way, you will not just be putting food on the table, but you will be feeding your spirit as well!

"We do not walk on our legs, but on our will."

-Sufi proverb

Eight Core Beliefs Underlying this Guide

The ideas, concepts and suggestions presented throughout this guide are based on the following beliefs. As you read them, consider the extent to which you agree or disagree with each item.

1. **Livelihood is a journey, not a destination. You plan to use this job so that it works on your behalf in the present and for your future.**

   A premise of this book is that you plan to use this job to get where you want to go. This job is not a final destination – no job is! In fact, through the use of the ideas in this guide, you may shape this job into one that you intend to stick with for a very long time and make yourself a very valuable contributor so that the employer may never want you to go. Either way – you can make this job work for you and on behalf of your livelihood.

"It's never too late to be what you might have been."

- George Ernst

2. **Any job you do is worth doing well.**

   No matter what you do or what position you are in, the second premise of this guide is that you want to give it your best effort because every day of your life is worth your best effort. Like they say in show business: There are no small parts, only small actors. There is no job too unworthy of doing well.

The most important job you'll ever have is to live your life fully.

3. **You'll get as much from your job as you are willing to put into it.**

   Many people are under the false assumption that work is supposed to bring them satisfaction, joy, purpose and challenge as well a paycheck. That is like believing that a relationship is supposed to bring you love, intimacy and excitement. If you've ever been in a relationship, you know that it is the people involved who have to bring love, intimacy and excitement *to* the relationship, not the other way around. It is the same with a job. You must bring purpose to your work if you expect to reap purposefulness from the job. (Actually the same is true of this little guide. The ideas presented will be only as powerful as the power you use to put them into action.)

   "Live your life each day as you would climb a mountain.
   An occasional glance toward the summit keeps
   the goal in mind, but many beautiful scenes
   are to be observed from each new vantage point.
   Climb slowly, steadily, enjoying each passing moment;
   and the view from the summit will serve
   as a fitting climax for the journey."

   - Harold Melchert

4. **Attitude matters!**

   As any great card player will tell you, success in life comes not from holding a good hand, but from playing a poor hand well. We do not have control over the hand we are dealt, but we are in control of how we play the hand.

Life is basically a self-fulfilling prophecy. It's not your boss, your job or the events happening in your life that create your reality. It's you. How you think and how you respond to these events is totally up to you.

During every moment of your life, you program your attitude to work for you or against you. Whatever your objectives and goals are, their direction is set by your attitude. Whether your thoughts are positive or negative, true or false, right or wrong, your attitude greatly colors your feelings and experience. This guide will help you steer your thoughts in a way that will work for you rather than against you.

5. **It is the small, daily choices you make that determine and shape your destiny.**

The quality of your experience in this new job will have as much to do with the daily choices you make as with anything else. It is important to keep your thoughts and energy focused on areas where you have control. This guide will help you to see the choices you have to make and to lay out options for making those choices.

It is said that people can be divided into three groups: those who make things happen, those who watch things happen, and those who wonder, "What happened?" This guide provides information to help you become part of the group that makes things happen by taking small, achievable steps every day.

6. **Successful employees treat their employers as customers, not caretakers.**

Think of a few places where you are a customer, like a video store, an auto shop or a restaurant. How can these places be assured that you will not take your business elsewhere? If you are like most customers, it depends upon the business' ability to meet your needs as a customer - it depends on the quality of their service.

"Do not go where the path leads. Rather, go your own way and leave a trail.""

   - Nicaraguan saying

"Genius is just perseverance in disguise."

   - Anonymous

The same is true of employment. No one owes you a job any more than you owe a restaurant your business. They earn the right to have you as a customer and as an employee you must continually earn the right to work for the employer. Of course, it is a two-way relationship and employers now know that in order to keep good employees they must look at their own workers as "internal customers."

Our job is to make life worth living! The same is true for one's work.

There is no such thing as job security in today's market, but that doesn't mean that you can't work to make your job more secure! The way that you do that is by treating your employer as a customer rather than a caretaker. This means changing your questions from "How secure is my job and is my employer going to take care of me?" to "How do I make myself valuable to this workplace? What does my employer need, want and expect from me and how can I exceed those expectations?" This guide will help you find hundreds of little ways to increase your security in the job by increasing your value to the employer!

"The important things in life cannot be gotten in advance. They must be gathered up fresh every day."

- George Regas

7. **Success on the job is related to skills and behaviors that are learnable.**

You have the qualifications to succeed on the job or you would not have been hired in the first place. Keeping the job has less to do with your qualifications and more to do with your personal qualities, social skills and other work behaviors. This guide highlights 30 specific skills that will set you apart and allow you to shine!

8. **You want more from work than a paycheck.**

Every person in the workforce has the right and the ability to find joy in their work. Life is just too short and too precious for us to "do time" in a job. Every job can and should work on behalf of the worker! In order for this to happen, however, it takes the will of the employee. This guide provides a way.

For most people, surviving the workday is their greatest concern. They float along in their daily lives like a piece of driftwood floating on the ocean. They take whatever job comes along and exert the least amount of energy possible to get the job done. They focus on lunch breaks, payday, and punching out at 5 o'clock. They feel like the job is an interruption between weekends. For employees with this survival focus, we recommend this guide in order to refocus their attention on "shining" in a job and enjoying the many rewards that will result. This guide instills the belief that work is not just about making a living, but about making a life! These 30 skills are not for those who are looking to survive – they are for those who want to thrive!

"I would rather be ashes than dust.

I would rather that my spark

Should burn out in a brilliant blaze

Than it would be stifled and dry-rot.

The proper function of man is to live, not exist.

I shall not waste my time in trying to prolong my days.

I shall use my time."

— Jack London

SKILL 1: CALMING NEW EMPLOYEE JITTERS
Think Progress, Not Perfection

Six Things to Remember To Deal with New Employee Jitters

If you are feeling a little uptight and nervous about being in a new place and new on the job, don't worry - it comes with the territory. Soon enough what feels "new" will feel "old hat". *Time on the job* is the only cure - luckily, it is reliable and quick-acting! In the words of every wise person who has ever lived, "This too shall pass."

"All I can do is let this day come in peace. All I can do is take the step before me now."

- Hugh Prather

1. **You're not in a contest!**

   If you are feeling unsure about your ability to do things right, to prove yourself and to look good in comparison to everyone else, remember that the very fact you got the job means you have already won the employer's confidence. You've earned the job offer so there is nothing here to win or to prove - now you're here to work!

2. **The only thing you have to prove is that you are teachable!**

   There are only two things you need to demonstrate to your employer at this stage of the game. They are:

   a. You are an eager learner and

   b. You are not afraid to admit what you do not know.

   If you can show that you are teachable, you are half way there!

You only grow by coming to the end of something and by beginning something else. This process is called living.

3. **80% of success is just showing up!**

There are two ways to show that you are teachable and both are things that are in your control to do: *Show up and listen!* Woody Allen once said that 80% of success is showing up! The other 20% is *being there* once you arrive! Showing up means listening, seeing, observing and following instructions. (Have you ever tried talking to someone who you knew was on another planet even though the person was right in front of you?)

4. **You are incomparable!**

I can hear you now, "Okay, so I don't have to prove myself to be anything but an eager learner and I have to show up and listen. But I'm still concerned about how I'm going to come across compared to others!" That brings us to some more great news:

YOU DON'T HAVE TO WORRY ABOUT COMPARING YOURSELF WITH ANYONE BECAUSE YOU ARE INCOMPARABLE!

At other times in your life you've probably been taught that in order to succeed, you have to do better than the other guy. But in the work world, you are not competing with your co-workers, you're playing on the same team! What the employer cares about is how the company looks in comparison to its competitors - not how you look! The employer hired you because they know that *you've got what it takes to succeed in your job*, and that's the only job that deserves your attention.

5. **Focus on progress, not perfection!**

Only you can truly know what progress means for you because you're the only one who knows where you are starting from! For some, progress may mean getting to work on time in a clean uniform, parking in a legal spot and making it to the end of the day without breaking out in hives. For someone else, progress means learning two new functions on the computer and then being able to use these

"Try not to become a person of success, but rather a person of value."

- Albert Einstein

"We rise to great heights by a winding staircase of small steps."

- Francis Bacon

"He who would learn to fly one day must first learn to stand and walk and run and climb and dance: One cannot fly into flying."

- Freidrich Neitzsche

skills with ease. Naturally, the company you work for will be holding you to their own set of standards and that is fair - it is part of the deal. They pay you and you follow their rules. But what I am talking about is your own expectations of yourself as you learn their rules. Because you are not perfect, you cannot expect perfection. But how about progress? That you can count on!

6. Measure Your Progress Bit by Bit!

Abraham Lincoln once noted that "the best thing about the future is that it only comes one day at a time." So maybe that's how we should live it. You know that you can't eat a pizza in one bite; it has to be eaten one bite at a time just as a book is read page by page and a house is built brick by brick. We accept the "bit by bit" nature of most things in life except when it comes to our own lives! We want instant success! In fact, we want it yesterday! This guide is going to prevent you from being overwhelmed by offering daily suggestions "bit by bit."

*"Man, like a bridge,
was destined to carry the load of the moment,
not the combined weight of a week,
month or year all at once."*

- William A. Ward

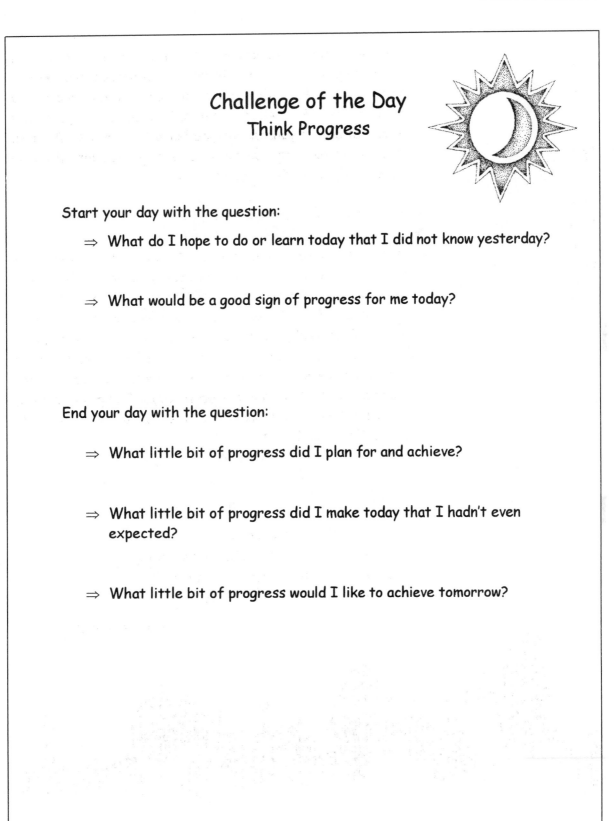

Challenge of the Day
Think Progress

Start your day with the question:

⇒ What do I hope to do or learn today that I did not know yesterday?

⇒ What would be a good sign of progress for me today?

End your day with the question:

⇒ What little bit of progress did I plan for and achieve?

⇒ What little bit of progress did I make today that I hadn't even expected?

⇒ What little bit of progress would I like to achieve tomorrow?

Shine

Your past cannot be changed,
but you can change tomorrow
by your actions today.

SKILL 2: DEALING WITH CHANGE
Prepare For The Winding Road Of Transition

Welcome to one of the most common roads in adult life – the Winding Road of Transition! You have been here before, no doubt, although you may not have seen its name on a signpost. It probably feels familiar if you have ever gone through any of the following life changes:

- Started a new school
- Moved to a new town
- Got married
- Got divorced, been separated
- Left or entered a new relationship
- Had parents who divorced or re-married
- Started a family or had a baby
- Suffered the loss of a loved one
- Changed jobs

"What lies behind us and what lies before us are tiny matters compared to what lies within us."

- Ralph Waldo Emerson

What all these experiences have in common is that they represent a major change, good or bad, in people's lives. What most people don't realize is that these changes also require us to go through *transition,* or a set of stages *(curves in the road)* that lead to change *(a point of new beginning).*

Starting a new job definitely counts as one of those changes that sets us on a winding road! Just as in driving on a real road, it helps us to steer and maneuver on the highway if we have some familiarity with the road, or at least a map to see where we are and where we are headed.

"He who is outside the door has a good part of his journey behind him."

- Dutch proverb

The diagram on the next page describes the curves in the road you can expect when adjusting to a new job. What follows are seven hot Traveling Tips for the Winding Road of Transition and a Challenge of the Day to help you make your way from one curve to the other until the road straightens out and you are feeling at home!

Map of Transition to a New Job

STAGE 1

Lost in the forest. (The road is curving so that you cannot see what is behind you or what lies ahead!)

You'll know when you are in this stage if you can relate to one or more of the following statements:

⇒ I am feeling strange about the new environment.

⇒ I don't know exactly how to be or what to do.

⇒ People are laughing at things I don't understand.

⇒ There seem to be a million things going on all at once and I'm finding it hard to focus.

⇒ I want to make a good impression but I feel like I'd be lucky to survive the week.

⇒ No one else seems to be lost like I am. They're making it look so easy.

STAGE 2

Finding your bearings (The road is curvy but not so wild!)

You'll know when you are in this stage if you can relate to one or more of the following statements:

⇒ I am faking it.

⇒ I am doing what I think I should do and punting from there.

⇒ I am watching and learning from other people.

⇒ Sometimes I feel like I am starting to get the hang of it and sometimes I don't.

⇒ I'm starting to get used to being a beginner.

⇒ Little by little I feel myself starting to adjust and I am not sticking out like a sore thumb.

STAGE 3
Thinking you are either in Heaven or in Hell. (You are going through a valley!)

You'll know when you are in this stage if you can relate to one or more of the following statements:

⇒ I love this place - this is great!

⇒ I feel like I am on an employment honeymoon!

⇒ I have found my people!

⇒ Where has this job been all my life?

Or

⇒ I hate this place!

⇒ I am so bored!

⇒ These people are bizarre!

⇒ I don't belong here!

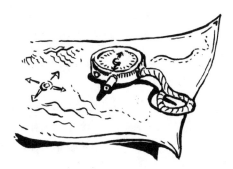

STAGE 4
You are adjusting. (The road is straightening out.)

You'll know when you are in this stage if you can relate to one or more of the following statements:

⇒ Well, it's not as good as I thought but I can deal with the disappointment.

⇒ I think the honeymoon is over but the marriage might be okay.

⇒ I may have gotten a little over-excited, but this is cool.

Or

⇒ Gee, it's not as bad as I thought, I think I can do this.

⇒ These folks are bizarre; but then, I'm a little strange myself.

⇒ This is different than I expected but I'm starting to get used to it.

Traveling Tips for the Winding Road of Transition

> "*E*ven when all else seems lost, the future still remains."
>
> - Nelson Mandela

1. **Mark your spot on the map.**

   Identify the stage you're in so you know what to expect! If you are feeling a little blue, and you realize that you are in the second stage of transition, you might say to yourself, "Hey, it's normal to feel down because I'm still feeling lost. It will pass when I begin to feel at home here. What can I do to feel better about it today?" Which of the four stages of transition do you relate to most right now?

2. **Check your rearview mirror!**

   Expectations can lead to disappointment and assumptions can get you into real trouble. What are some of the pictures you had of yourself in this job? How did you imagine this place to feel? How do you think your pictures match with the employer's pictures? Do you think you and the employer have the same expectations?

3. **Keep your eye on the road.**

   Focus on what is going right. Don't lose your concentration by trying to pay attention to the million and one things going on around you. Keep your energy and effort in the place where you feel you have some control and continue to remind yourself of what is working out well so far.

> "*T*he world is round. The place which may seem like an end may also be a beginning."
>
> - Anonymous

4. **Know the rules of the road.**

   Clarify what is expected of you from other people as quickly as possible. Who do you have to please? What do you have to do to please them? How will you know if you have done what they expect? If you cannot answer these questions, find someone who can respond to them. They will respect you for asking!

5. Share the road!

You don't have to go the distance alone. Everyone around you has gone through (or is going through) something similar when they started their job. Most people are thrilled to be asked for support! It is a compliment, a sign of respect and an invitation to friendship. If you do not have people to support you outside of work, find a mentor or a co-worker who is willing to be supportive.

6. Take the journey one mile at a time.

You don't harvest a garden overnight and you won't find your groove in your new job overnight. Consider it a project that you work on a bit every day.

7. Bring several pairs of sunglasses!

Your mind is wonderfully versatile. Like changing sunglasses with blue lens to yellow, you can change the lens from which you view the world from dark to light, fearful to hopeful. Find and hold to a perspective that makes sense of this transition and helps you keep a sense of humor. W.C. Fields once said that "Life is a tragedy up close and but a comedy seen from a distance." The same thing that can make us cry, seen through another lens, can make us laugh. What you need is the ability to see things through various lenses. Following this guide will help you do that!

"Skillful pilots gain their reputation from tempests and from storms. Staying the course is all that matters."

- Epicurus

"The only courage you need is the kind that gets you from moment to moment."

- Krishnamurti

Challenge of the Day
Coping with Transition

1. Ask your supervisor at the end of the day:

   "How am I doing? Can you give me a few hints
   on how I could be doing better?"

2. You need support while going through this transition. Make a list of friends and acquaintances in whose company you feel more alive, happy and optimistic. Choose one with whom you will spend some time this week.

3. FOOD FOR THE SOUL: Because you are in the beginning stages of transition at work, you need to feel the comfort of home in other parts of your life. Do something special for yourself every day after work that reinforces the parts of your life where you feel comfortable and in control. For example, read to your kids, go for a walk in your neighborhood, cook your favorite meal, or call your best friend.

SKILL 3: UNDERSTANDING WORKPLACE CULTURE
When In Rome, Do As The Romans Do

Travel around the world and you will quickly learn one thing - every country has its own culture. Across cultures you will see differences in everything from laws, language, religion, dress, food, holidays, and God forbid, even driving rules. The same is true on a smaller level within families. Every household has its own culture - its own unwritten rules and expectations about relating, behaving and sharing a home together. (For proof, observe differences in table manners at the homes of friends and relatives, or even, the T.V. controller etiquette.)

"All of life is a stage."

- William Shakespeare

Workplaces have their own cultures too. Some companies let employees come to work in their blue jeans while others expect employees to wear suits or uniforms. In some offices you will see employees throw spitballs at each other from across the room while in others such behavior will get you sent straight to the principal, excuse me, CEO. In some you will hear the constant laughter and bantering of co-workers while in others you will not hear even the stirring of a mouse. Workplaces are like their own countries - it's just that you can't buy a guide to their cross-cultural differences.

Unfortunately, as a new employee, you do not have the luxury of time to stumble across the many cultural rules of your new workplace. In order to increase your likelihood of success on the job and acceptance by the workgroup, go in with your eyes open - learn the unwritten rules. Before you can "do as the Romans do" - you need to *know* what they do!

Throughout this guide I will point out different aspects of the company culture for you to pay attention to and questions for you to ask. But in this first week of work there are a few aspects of the workplace that you need to know about NOW - like the dress code, the use of personal equipment, everyday employee protocol and dealing with unusual circumstances.

Challenge of the Day
Learn the Unwritten Rules

Use the forms on the next four pages to guide you in "getting the scoop" on your company's culture. People you might go to for this information include co-workers, a mentor or a supervisor.

Dress Code

Imagine how the dress code varies from a bar, a doctor's office, a software company and a lumber mill. Employee dress codes vary not only from industry to industry, but from one workplace to another within the same industry! (For example, most airlines require flight attendants to don blue and white uniforms with scarves tied neatly around their necks while the attendants at Southwest Airlines jump around in khaki shorts and T-shirts!) As an employee, you are paid not only to do the work but also to carry the image of the company. Naturally, how you come across is affected not just by what you wear, but how you fix your hair, wear your make-up, your nails, etc. Inquiring minds would want to know the do's and don'ts in each of the following categories.

Clothing/uniform:

Shoes and socks or stockings:

Jewelry and accessories:

Tattoos and body piercing:

Nails:

Hair:

Make-Up:

Personal Hygiene:

Personal Use of Equipment and Resources

Is it okay to use the telephone to make a personal call on your break? Can you fax your registration to the DMV over lunch? Is it kosher to pour yourself coffee any time you want? Can you slip the pens with the company logo into the Christmas stockings of friends and family? The truth is – you don't know until you ask. But until you do, **assume it is not okay.** Assuming it is fine to do something when it is not can get you fired. Ask for the do's and don'ts in the categories below.

Personal Telephone Calls:

Computer:

Fax machine:

E-mail:

Printer or copier:

Supplies:

Food and/or Drink:

Other:

Everyday Employee Protocol

Does starting at 8:00 AM mean you need to get there at 7:45 AM because your first customer will be in your face at 8:02 AM or do you get 15 minutes to "open up"? Is lunch a quick break to eat or is it a chance to get some errands done? Can you smoke anywhere on the premises? Is it okay to listen to your discman while working on the line? Who empties the garbage can and where? Here are some questions regarding "unwritten rules" that are important for you to know.

What do you need to do when you check in or start your shift?

What are your options for lunch time? Can you bring a lunch? Is there a microwave, refrigerator, or cafeteria? What restaurants or food stores are in the area?

What are the Do's and Don'ts with regard to:

Taking breaks:

Parking:

Smoking:

Eating and drinking:

Listening to music:

Use of employee lounge or other areas:

Other:

Dealing with Unusual Circumstances (They better be unusual)

Can you change your schedule in order to make a doctor's appointment? How about an AA meeting? What if you need to take your dog to the vet? (That probably depends on whether or not your employer is a pet owner!) What if someone in your family is very ill - can you take some time off?

Once again - the rules differ from workplace to workplace. Therefore, it is critical that you find out what the rules are where you work. Until you know them, play it safe, that way you will not be disappointed (or fired) by your assumptions and you might just be pleasantly surprised! Here is what you need to find out.

What are acceptable and unacceptable reasons for absence from work?

What are acceptable and unacceptable reasons for tardiness?

What are the three most common causes for people getting fired from this workplace?

How do you know if you've blown it? What are the signs?

Find out what you need to know about the following:

Calling in sick:

Getting time off:

Changing your work schedule:

Needing to come in late or leave work early:

What are three most common workplace injuries and how do I avoid them?

What do I do if I get injured on the job?

Who do I go to if I need help or have a question?

SKILL 4: MEETING NEW PEOPLE
Take Advantage Of A Clean Slate

If you could choose how people in your workplace describe you six weeks from now, what would you have them saying about you? What words would you have them use to describe you as a person or as a co-worker? Circle two or three words from the list below or write a few of your own in the space below.

"I always wanted to be somebody, I guess I should have been more specific!"

- Lily Tomlin

Assertive	**Motivated**	**Open-minded**	**Outgoing**
Cheerful	**Patient**	**Independent**	**Sincere**
Reliable	**Dependable**	**Skillful**	**Eager**
Committed	**Helpful**	**Funny**	**Creative**
Fun to be around	**Easy-going**	**Enthusiastic**	**Energetic**
Friendly	**Sensitive**	**Trustworthy**	**Interesting**

Other words:

Now consider *what you could do or how you could act* in the next six weeks that would cause people to use those words to describe you? The truth is, if you act in accordance with the words you circled and wrote above, you will get your wish. If you want to be seen as trustworthy . . . don't break a trust and prove that you are able to keep a secret. If you want to be described as helpful, find ways of reaching out to help people.

HOT TIP: Take advantage of a clean slate: *Live* the image you want people to have of you! Drop any survival habits that no longer serve you – whether it be a hard shell, a tough guy act, or using your looks rather than your brains.

Here's the cool thing - You are making brand new relationships! You have no history with people at your new job, you are working from a clean slate. Like an artist working on a blank canvas, you are starting from scratch with people and you can create the image you want people to have of you. On the next page you will find a list of suggestions for meeting new people at work and starting relationships on the right foot.

Suggestions for Starting
Relationships Off on the Right Foot

Place a check next to each suggestion that you think is worth taking and that you will put into immediate practice.

_____ 1. Make a habit of introducing yourself to people you don't know by saying something like,

> *"Hi! My name is Joe. I just started*
> *here a few days ago as a stock clerk.*
> *What do you do?"   or*

> *"How are you doing? I'm Sarah.*
> *I'm the new receptionist.*
> *What department are you in?"*

_____ 2. Make everyone you meet feel important by giving them your full attention. (Shake hands with people who offer theirs and offer to shake hands with other people if you are comfortable doing so.)

_____ 3. Listen and learn people's names. It's one of the most important tributes you can pay another person. If it is a foreign name, repeat it and ask if you have pronounced it correctly. What a wonderful way to show respect to another person!

_____ 4. Do not assume that people want to be called by their first name. Ask permission to call the person by their first name.

_____ 5. Greet people in the workplace with a smile. Even on the telephone, smile with your voice.

_____ 6. When someone compliments you, say thank you and accept the praise. (Never interrupt people who are flattering you!) When someone welcomes you to the company, express that you are glad to be part of the team.

"If you are not using your smile, you're like a man with a million dollars in the bank and no checkbook."

- Les Giblin

_____ 7. As you work with co-workers or customers today, think about what you could do to make the customer glad they were served by you or your co-worker.

_____ 8. Don't try to impress anyone today - just be impressed by everyone else!

_____ 9. Be careful of what information you pass on to other people. Not everything someone tells you is meant to be repeated to others. Let people know that they can trust you with their confidences.

_____ 10. Be *service-oriented* rather than *self-oriented*. Show your interest in other people's concerns, not just your own.   When you have someone else's interest at heart, they can feel it and will be drawn to you. Ask a question like, "As a receptionist, what can I do to make your job easier? Is there anything in particular you would like me to communicate to your callers?" or "When people drop their cars off here, what do you think they like to hear?"

_____ 11. If someone speaks another language and you do not understand the person, don't fake it – ask for clarification. This shows respect and says that what they have to say is important enough for you to ask again.

_____ 12. Look at the image you are presenting to other people not just through your words, but how you dress, your appearance, the way you walk, sit and stand.   Look in the mirror and ask, "Am I presenting the person that fits the words I circled on the previous page?" As unfair as it may be, people judge you by the way you look. Do the best with what you have. Go to work clean and neat.

"Each friend opens a world in us, a world possibly not born until they arrive, and it is only by this meeting that a new world is born."

- Anais Nin

____ 13. Focus on the person in front of you rather than compare him or her to other people you have known. Avoid the tendency to stereotype people. Every person deserves to be treated as an individual rather than as a member of group.

____ 14. As you meet new people, assume or at least remain open to the possibility that this person may be the opening to a whole new world in you. Meet people expecting to like them!

Challenge of the Day
Meet New People

1. Introduce yourself to three new people today. Focus on remembering their names.

2. Think about one person you have met on the job who didn't make a good impression on you. Give the person the benefit of the doubt and try seeing him or her "fresh" today - free of your pre-conceptions.

3. Write down one quality or characteristic for which you would like to be known. Decide how you can create that image and then an action that supports it. Carry a symbol of some kind or put something on your desk which reminds you to live the quality that you want others to see in you. (For example, if you want people to see you as "grounded", carry a small rock in your pocket. If you want to try being more "easy-going" cut out a small picture of a creek or a river to hang in your personal work space.)

    Quality/Characteristic   Action   Symbol

4. Send a thank you note or find some other way to thank and recognize people who helped you secure this job.

SKILL 5: SATISFYING EMPLOYER EXPECTATIONS
Fifteen Key Behaviors

Once upon a time a man wished so deeply to win the lottery that he knelt down and prayed, "Dear Lord I have been a good man, please let me win the lottery!" He had faith and arose the next day with great anticipation. Nothing happened. No phone call. No knock at the door. That night he knelt down again and prayed the same prayer. Again, the next day nothing happened. On the third night as he prayed, "Please Lord, do you hear me? I really want to win the lottery!", he heard a voice from the heavens declare, "Give me a break, Buddy! Why don't you meet me half way and buy yourself a ticket!"

This story speaks to the role of "action" in the attainment of anything we desire. Fortunately, the desire to achieve success on the job is not a matter of luck or fate; rather, it largely depends on everyday choices you make and behaviors you exhibit. The list on the next page represents typical behaviors business owners expect of their employees. Follow the instructions in the Challenge of the Day to assess the behaviors you may need to develop more fully so that they are simply a matter of habit.

Challenge of the Day

(a) Please place a check (✓) next to each item on the Employee Behavior Checklist that you would expect of employees if you were an employer;

(b) Place a star (✶) next to each of the behaviors that come naturally to you – the behaviors that will not require any forethought or effort on your part; and,

(c) Circle those behaviors that may be difficult for you to adjust to and/or remember.

Employee Behavior Checklist

(1) _____   Following company rules and regulations.

(2) _____   Showing up for work on time; calling in promptly when late or sick.

(3) _____   Having good personal hygiene (coming to work clean) and dressing appropriately.

(4) _____   Relating to co-workers and customers in a professional manner.

(5) _____   Managing your moods and emotions appropriately (not getting angry or emotional on the job).

(6) _____   Being willing to speak up when there is a problem and admit when you've made a mistake.

(7) _____   Being able to respond well to constructive criticism and learning from feedback.

(8) _____   Treating co-workers with respect; not swearing, flirting with or teasing co-workers or telling racist or sexist jokes.

(9) _____   Looking for ways to use time, skills and talents to the advantage of the organization; not waiting for someone else to tell you what to do but seeking ways to maintain productivity.

(10) _____   Meeting performance goals and standards.

(11) _____   Being willing to share and give credit where credit is due.

(12) _____   Being honest regarding hours worked.

(13) _____   Being loyal to the company in terms of not sharing product or service secrets or customers with competitors.

(14) _____   Not lying, cheating or stealing from the company, one's co-workers or customers.

(15) _____   Not drinking alcohol or using drugs during work hours; not coming to work having consumed alcohol or drugs.

List the behaviors that you circled below. For each, identify two or three things you can do to increase your effectiveness in these areas until they become "natural" to you.

Behavior   **Actions/Reminders/Ideas**

SKILL 6: LEARNING TO RELATE IN THE COMPANY STYLE
Dance With Wolves

QUESTION OF THE DAY:
What do the shows "Dances with Wolves", "Crocodile Dundee" and "Mork and Mindy" have in common?

Well, okay, they all had famous actors. What else? They all had a pretty love interest, yeah, yeah. Here's a hint: the main character in each of these shows faced a similar dilemma . . . what was it? Time's Up: They each had to relate to a world that was totally foreign to them. Of course, Kevin Costner's character pulls it off much better than that of Paul Hogan or of Robin Williams who inspired a whole generation to greet each other with "Nanu Nanu". Can you think of other films where people had to learn to relate in a new way?

On a more practical level, have you ever noticed that the way Italians talk to each other is very different from the Japanese? How different is it being greeted in a fancy restaurant versus a fast food joint? How do the large car dealers answer their phones differently than the mom and pop auto-shop on the corner? Let's face it - we needn't get passports and travel the world to enter different realities - we simply need to enter the work world.

Earlier you looked at several aspects of your employer's company culture, including dress code, and written and unwritten rules. But today you are going to pay attention to another very important part of that culture - the way people relate to each other. What you do with that information is up to you. Will you be more like Mork and stand on your head when asked to take a chair or will you be more like Dances with Wolves and take a name like "Works like Beaver"?

Challenge of the Day
Relate in the Company Style

Use the questions on this page as a guide for what to watch, listen and ask about in relation to how people at your workplace relate to each other, to management and to customers or clients. Talk to a co-worker, a mentor or a supervisor for advice in any of those areas in which you feel unsure or uncomfortable. Jot down this information in your Daily Notes.

1. How do people address each other? Do certain individuals have titles you should be aware of?

2. Is it okay to call people by their first names?

3. What do we say when we answer the phones?

4. How do we greet customers or clientele?

5. How do co-workers greet each other?

6. Is this a high-touch culture with group hugs or do people nod their heads slightly when they are thrilled to see each other?

7. What are the customs of interruption? Can you just walk into a person's cubicle or do you have to knock?

8. Do employees socialize during lunch or dinner breaks?

9. Are there after-hours work functions? If so, what are they like?

10. How do employees interact here department to department, office to office or branch to branch?

11. How would you characterize the sense of humor of this workplace?

SKILL 7: CLARIFYING PERFORMANCE GOALS
Target Your Goals And Make Them Smart

Here is the classic formula for developing SMART work goals. See if you can answer these questions and if not, seek the answers from your supervisor or a mentor. The clearer your target is, the better your chances for hitting a bull's eye!

Specific

What do you do?
What are your specific goals?
When things are crazy at work, which tasks or goals should take priority?

Measurable

How will you know when you have met your goals?
How are they measured?
Can you break down large goals into smaller parts?
What are the signs along the way to larger goals that let you know you are working well?

Achievable

Do you feel capable of meeting these goals?
What do you need to do in terms of tools and/or training in order to perform your job?
When you need help along the way, where do you go?

Relevant

Why is your work important?
Who is it important to?
How does your work affect other people in the company?
How does it affect the customers?

Timely

What are the timelines for meeting your goals?
How do your daily goals differ from your weekly or monthly goals?

Challenge of the Day
Clarify Your Goals

1. Keep a victory log in your Daily Notes and write down every time you meet a goal.

2. Know that it is less important to get everything done than it is to get the most important things done. Ask your supervisor which jobs or tasks take priority when things get crazy at work.

3. Ask your supervisor how you should use your time when work is not very busy.

4. Ask your supervisor: "When I've been given orders from different people, how do I know which person to respond to first?"

5. FOOD FOR THE SOUL: Find one small job to complete at home. Whether it be to clean out your refrigerator or organize your bathroom cabinet, enjoy the satisfaction of completing one small job at home.

SKILL 8: PAYING ATTENTION TO YOUR SURROUNDINGS
Your Workplace As A Learning Place

What if you were to view everything that happens to you as your teacher? What if you looked at the ups, the downs, the pleasures and the challenges of your job as holding some kind of lesson to learn from? Buddha once said, "Imagine that every person in the world is enlightened but you. They are all your teachers, each doing just the right things to help you learn patience, perfect wisdom, perfect compassion."

In short, what if you could learn to sit at the feet of your life and be taught? That's what you're going to practice today – in your very own workplace! No matter what job you are in, think of it as being paid to learn. Put a check (✓) next to everything on the list below that you could learn in your present job:

_____ How to meet people and start new relationships

_____ How to solve problems

_____ How to learn

_____ How to communicate with customers

_____ How a business is run

_____ How employees relate to the employer

_____ What employers care about in the workplace

_____ How to budget and make the most of your wages

_____ How to use tools and equipment

_____ How people work as a team

_____ The ups and downs of the industry you are working in

_____ How to use your time well in juggling life and work

_____ What you like about the job and want more of in future work opportunities

_____ What you don't like about the job and want to avoid in future work opportunities

"Learning is the jewel casting brilliance into the future."

- Marie Evans

HOT TIP: Ask questions! Resolve to never stop being a student of life, a professional learner!

Challenge of the Day
Paying Attention

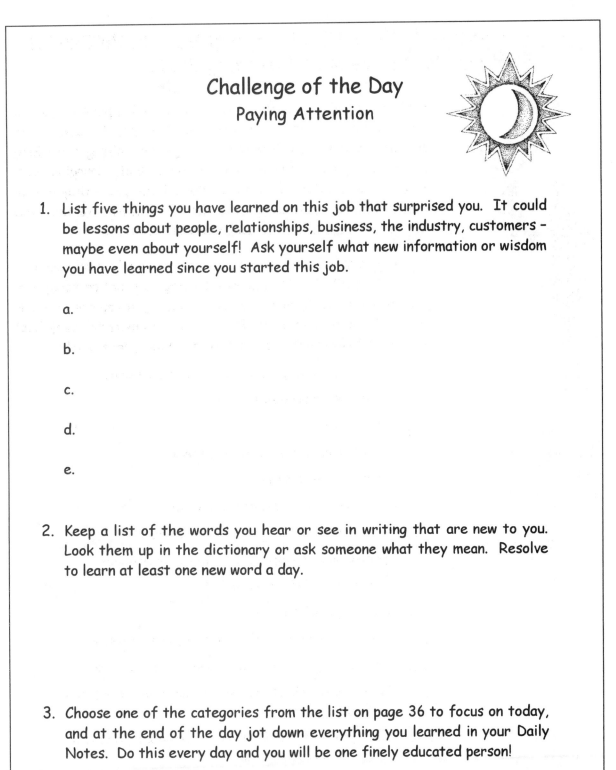

1. List five things you have learned on this job that surprised you. It could be lessons about people, relationships, business, the industry, customers – maybe even about yourself! Ask yourself what new information or wisdom you have learned since you started this job.

    a.

    b.

    c.

    d.

    e.

2. Keep a list of the words you hear or see in writing that are new to you. Look them up in the dictionary or ask someone what they mean. Resolve to learn at least one new word a day.

3. Choose one of the categories from the list on page 36 to focus on today, and at the end of the day jot down everything you learned in your Daily Notes. Do this every day and you will be one finely educated person!

SKILL 9: LEARNING FROM MISTAKES
Make Fresh Ones, Not The Same Ones

Making mistakes is a natural part of the learning process. The important thing is that we don't keep repeating the same ones over and over again - but that we learn from them and make fresh ones! In other words, if we're gonna fall, we might as well fall forward!

6 HOT TIPS FOR MAKING FRESH MISTAKES

1. Learn from your mistakes. Don't keep making the same ones over and over again. Emptying the coffee pot and leaving it on a hot burner will be easily forgiven the first time. By the second or third time those fumes hit the nostrils of your co-workers, you're in trouble.

2. When you make a mistake that really hurts someone else, use this painful situation to show just how teachable you really are. There is nothing like a sincere apology to show your true face. Avoid the temptation to run from the problem, run to it instead. Mistakes keep us humble and humility earns us respect. When making an apology, be sure to cover three things:

    • *What you are sorry about (how your actions affected the person);*

    • *How or why it happened (there is a big difference between an excuse and an explanation - excuses usually worsen the situation); and,*

    • *What you will do to make sure it doesn't happen again.*

3. Let your mistakes come from good intentions. If you are working, relating, and communicating from a good place, even your mistakes will carry the aura of your good intentions.

4. Don't expect that everyone will appreciate your mistakes as much as you do. That's okay. Their business is about accounting for their own mistakes. Be forgiving first. It really is contagious!

5. Expect to make at least one mistake a day in order to know you are still in the game of life. If you go to bed at night without being able to think of one experience you would do differently the next time, know that you are probably living too far from the edge or simply not paying attention.

6. Most problems can be transformed just by changing how you look at them. If you want a way to get rid of your present problems, just get yourself a bigger one. (For example, if you are having troubles on this job, quitting your job will create a bigger problem - No job at all!)

Challenge of the Day
Learn from Mistakes

1. List three mistakes you worry most about making on this job.
   a.

   b.

   c.

2. For each situation listed above, consider the following:
   - How can they be avoided?
   - What do you do if they happen?
   - What opportunities might you miss by trying to avoid these situations?

3. Think of the three mistakes you have made so far on this job. What did you learn? How did they help you "grow"?
   a.

   b.

   c.

4. Make an Apology.

   Everyone is good when things are going well . . . you show your truest colors when things have gone wrong. Is there anyone at work or at home to whom you owe an apology? If so, use this opportunity to shine and show how you can own up to a mistake.

5. Hang this saying somewhere in you personal work space:

   There is no such thing as failure, only feedback!

SKILL 10: NOT LETTING WORRY CRAMP YOUR STYLE
Adopt The Gretzky Approach To Making "GOALS"

"Statistically - 100% of the shots you don't take, don't go in."
                                    - Wayne Gretsky

True or False?

1. T___ F___ Most of what we worry about eventually happens.
2. T___ F___ Worry is one way of coping with the present.
3. T___ F___ Worrying is based on logic.
4. T___ F___ People who never worry are either unrealistic or idealistic.

On the contrary, most of what we worry about **never** happens! Worry is not about the present because all of our worries are based on thoughts of the future! Worry is not based on logic, it is based in our imaginations! Our mind can go one of two ways when we think about the future – it can go the way of hope or the way of fear.

Worry is nothing more than letting your imagination create its own fear-based picture of the future and then reacting to your picture as if it's real! Sound kind of crazy? That's because it is. Worse yet, it is wasted thought! I mean, if worrying worked – if it paid the bills, or solved a problem or prevented an illness, at least there'd be a good reason for doing it. But worrying does not keep the trouble out of tomorrow; it just keeps the joy out of today! Meanwhile, Life is begging us to grow and stretch our wings. Therefore take this advice, don't let worry clip your wings!

"Life is either a daring adventure – or it is nothing."

                                    - Helen Keller

"Do not be too timid or squeamish about your actions. All life is an experiment."

                                    - Ralph Waldo Emerson

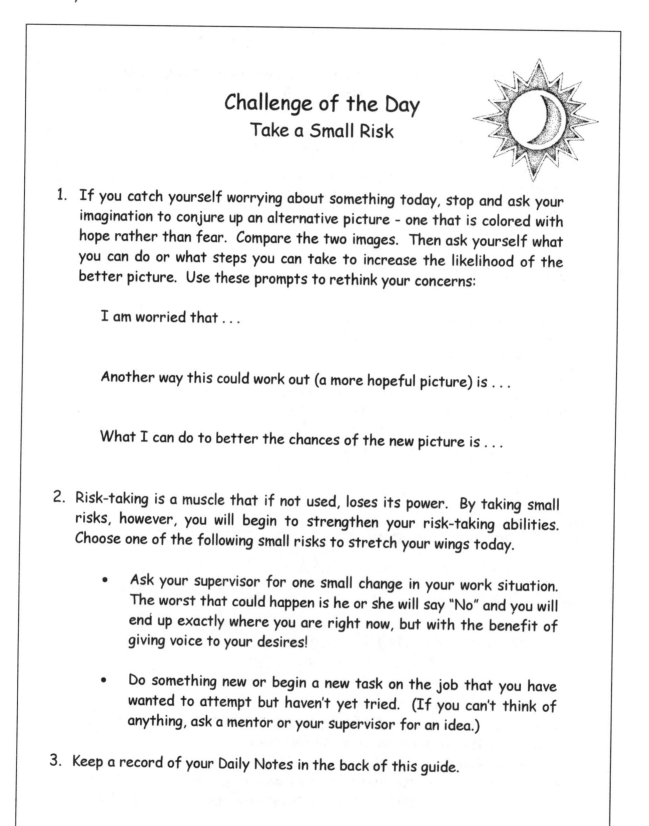

Challenge of the Day
Take a Small Risk

1. If you catch yourself worrying about something today, stop and ask your imagination to conjure up an alternative picture - one that is colored with hope rather than fear. Compare the two images. Then ask yourself what you can do or what steps you can take to increase the likelihood of the better picture. Use these prompts to rethink your concerns:

    I am worried that . . .

    Another way this could work out (a more hopeful picture) is . . .

    What I can do to better the chances of the new picture is . . .

2. Risk-taking is a muscle that if not used, loses its power. By taking small risks, however, you will begin to strengthen your risk-taking abilities. Choose one of the following small risks to stretch your wings today.

    *   Ask your supervisor for one small change in your work situation. The worst that could happen is he or she will say "No" and you will end up exactly where you are right now, but with the benefit of giving voice to your desires!

    *   Do something new or begin a new task on the job that you have wanted to attempt but haven't yet tried. (If you can't think of anything, ask a mentor or your supervisor for an idea.)

3. Keep a record of your Daily Notes in the back of this guide.

JOB SATISFACTION: SURVEY ONE

Please rate each statement from 1 to 4 using the following scale:
1 = Strongly Disagree   2 = Disagree   3 = Agree   4 = Strongly Agree

A: Performance Expectations and Workload

I know what is expected of me.	1	2	3	4
The priorities of my job are clear.	1	2	3	4
I know what I am doing right and what I am doing wrong.	1	2	3	4
I know what my supervisor thinks of my performance.	1	2	3	4
I know how to get the information I need to do my job	1	2	3	4
I have plenty to keep me busy at work.	1	2	3	4
This job is a good fit for my qualifications and skill-level.	1	2	3	4

B: Communication and Feedback

I don't have any problems with people here.	1	2	3	4
I feel able to communicate my needs and desires.	1	2	3	4
I know where to go when I have a problem.	1	2	3	4
I am not afraid of admitting when I make a mistake.	1	2	3	4
My supervisor gives me good feedback.	1	2	3	4

C: Teamwork and Belonging

I fit in here.	1	2	3	4
I work well with my co-workers.	1	2	3	4
I feel valued and respected here.	1	2	3	4
I feel like I am part of a real team.	1	2	3	4

D: Motivation and Personal Growth

My work is appreciated.	1	2	3	4
I am proud of what we do here.	1	2	3	4
I believe this job will help me progress in my vocational goals.	1	2	3	4
I enjoy my job and I like being at my workplace.	1	2	3	4
I am proud to tell people where I work and what I do.	1	2	3	4

E: Stress Management

I have enough time to do what I need to do at work.	1	2	3	4
I have confidence in myself to make the best of this situation.	1	2	3	4
I am able to make ends meet financially.	1	2	3	4
Personal problems are not interfering with my work life.	1	2	3	4
I have support systems in place to help me with personal issues.	1	2	3	4
I am taking good care of my health.	1	2	3	4

Date completed _____

SKILL 11: REFLECTING THE COMPANY IMAGE
Play To Your Audience

"There is only one thing every actor must remember that is more important than technique – and that's to play to your audience!"

- Dustin Hoffman

Playing to your audience is great advice not just for actors, musicians and other performance artists, but for every employee who is playing to the ultimate audience - the company they work for. The qualities you try to develop and the skills you sharpen should depend in great part on the needs and interests of your company. In the Challenge of the Day you will find a list of important questions that will help you discover how best to "play to your audience" - regardless of the position you are in.

By the way, not only will your employer enjoy answering these questions, completing this survey will better equip you to shine in the two skills that follow, Going the Extra Mile for the Employer and Shining in the Eyes of the Customer!

A Tale of Two Gas Stations

A man pumping gas at a filling station was asked why his station was always so busy while the one across the street selling comparable gas at an identical price was almost always empty. The wise businessman replied, "They are in a totally different business than us. They're a fillin' station – we're a service station!"

Challenge of the Day
Understand the Company Image

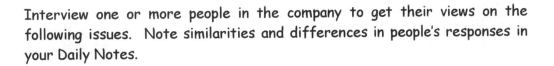

Interview one or more people in the company to get their views on the following issues. Note similarities and differences in people's responses in your Daily Notes.

1. What are three of the most valued worker traits of people in my position?

2. How would you describe a "star employee" of this workplace?

3. What is the reputation of this company by other players in the industry?

4. How does this company pride itself? What sets this company apart from its competitors?

5. What is considered "excellent service" at this company?

SKILL 12: EXCEEDING EMPLOYER EXPECTATIONS
Go The Extra Mile

"If a man is called to be a street sweeper, he should sweep streets even as Michelangelo painted, or Beethoven composed music, or Shakespeare wrote poetry. He should sweep streets so well that all the hosts of heaven and earth will pause to say, 'Here lived a street sweeper who did his job well.' "

- Martin Luther King, Jr.

"If you make your job important, it's likely to return the favor."

- Anonymous

There is no traffic in the extra mile!

Most people want to do their job well enough to keep it. But simply fulfilling the requirements of the job will not set you apart or make you shine. What Martin Luther King was talking about when he said we should work "as Michelangelo painted", is to go the extra mile. He is suggesting that you look beyond the confines of your job and find a way to demonstrate that "something extra". Today's Challenge of the Day will help you discover how you can do your work in a way that will impress, if not all the hosts of heaven and earth, at least your supervisor, your co-workers or your customers. Here is a list of great suggestions to spark your creative thinking about how to make your mark.

Suggestions for Going the Extra Mile for Your Employer

1. Do more than you are asked and contribute more than what is required.

2. **When performing routine tasks, make it your first time.**

To prevent boredom, when faced with a routine task – typing letters, answering the telephone, filling out forms, washing and clearing the tables, making a presentation - approach each task as if it were your first time. Each letter, each call, each customer is, after all, different. So rather than see the individual assignments as a lump of indistinguishable work, handle each one with a fresh mind. After all, while you may have poured a hundred cups of coffee or called 20 other people today, it is always the first time for the customer!

"In a gentle way you can shake the world."

- Mahatma Gandhi

3. **If you don't have anything to do, find something to do.**

Never find yourself idle during working hours. If you cannot find something to do, ask your supervisor for a list of suggestions of how you can best use your time when things are slow.

"Whatever you do - do it big, do it right and do it with style!"

- Fred Astaire

4. **Look for ways to save your manager, office, department, or team time and money.**

For example, a stock clerk in a electronics part store could suggest that when things are slow in the mornings, she could assemble customer orders so that the lines move faster in the afternoon hours. Suggest that regular customers send in a product list that you will have ready when they arrive.

5. **Look for additional ways for your employer to make more money or capitalize on its customer base.**

For example, an employee at a toy store could suggest adding to his job description the service of assembling items which come unassembled; or an attendant of valet parking at a hotel can suggest that for an added fee to the customer, he could wash their cars.

"Every job is a self-portrait of the person who did it. Autograph your work with excellence!"

- Anonymous

"If a man writes a better book, preaches a better sermon, or makes a better mouse-trap than his neighbor, though his house be deep in the woods, the world will make a beaten path to his door."

- Ralph Waldo Emerson

6. **Volunteer to do the things that seem to fall between the cracks that you don't mind doing anyway.**

   For example, emptying the trash before you check out, laundering uniforms, distributing faxes as they start to pile up, answering the phones while someone is on a break, etc.

7. **Make a game of your work in a way that improves it.**

   For example, the telemarketer may try surpassing a self-imposed quota of 20 calls per hour, a nursing assistant may set out to discover new ways to make her patients laugh, or a busperson may try to set a new record for getting a table cleaned and reset.

8. **Commit as much of yourself as possible to what you are doing in each moment.**

   This follows the Buddhist advice, "When chopping wood, chop wood. When carrying water, carry water." In your mind, don't be in your car driving home when you're supposed to be attending to a customer. Give your full attention to your work.

9. **Offer to learn a new task or process you can share with the people in your department or area.**

   For example, the computer operator who learned to build the company's website or the child care worker who learned beginning sign language in order to communicate better with a deaf parent.

10. **Look for chronic problems in your area that have been ignored and work on generating solutions.**

    For example, the cosmetologist who offered to serve customers in their homes during the evenings so as not to lose business from those working full time during the day.

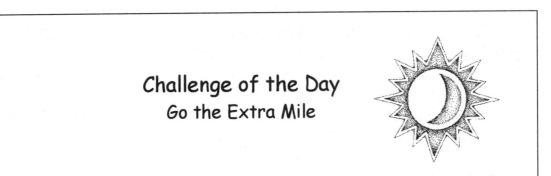

Challenge of the Day
Go the Extra Mile

1. Using the suggestions listed, identify at least three ways that you can begin going the extra mile for your employer:

    a.

    b.

    c.

2. Ask a supervisor, mentor or co-worker for suggestions on how you might go the extra mile.

3. Follow the suggestions you listed above for the next five days. Write in your Daily Notes how you feel when you stretch yourself as an employee. Jot down all the benefits you can think of for going the extra mile.

"Great opportunities to help others seldom come,
but small ones surround us daily."

- Sally Koch

SKILL 13: SHINING IN THE EYES OF THE CUSTOMER
Roll Out The Carpet In Service

Here is a simple but powerful rule:

Always give people more than they expect!

"Hold yourself to a higher standard than anybody else expects of you."

- Henry Ward Beecher

Among the many benefits of putting that rule into practice is the fact that you will shine in the eyes of your customers! In most businesses, the only real way to differentiate yourself from the competition is through service. Paying attention to the needs of your customers and finding a way to make them feel special is a powerful business advantage. Here are three ways to surprise your customers with service that will put a smile on their faces and make your work that much more fulfilling and fun!

1. **Pay attention to the needs of your customers that go beyond basic service.**

   As customers we want more than the basic service. Beyond having our car washed, our hair styled, or our computers repaired, we want to feel welcomed, understood, listened to and respected. It doesn't matter what kind of business you are in, your customers' basic human needs must be met.

What other needs does the customer have in your business beyond mere service? For example, we expect an amusement park to be cheerful, clean and family-oriented while from the dentist's office we expect individual attention and professional care.

The Needs of Customers in Your Business

Circle the words below which you think reflect the needs and expectations of customers in your business.

Accuracy	Elegant	Pleasant
Availability	Experienced	Professional
Caring	Entertaining	Relaxing
Clean	Fair	Reliable
Comfortable	Fast	Respectful
Competitive	Flexible	Safe
Convenience	Friendly	Sincere
Consistent	Helpful	Timeliness
Cost effective	Innovative	Trustworthy
Customized	Knowledgeable	Understanding
Dependable	Low cost	Unique
Easy to use	On time	Up scale
Effective	Personal	Warm

Others:

"All work that uplifts humanity, even a small way, has dignity and importance and should be undertaken with excellence."

- Martin Luther King, Jr.

2. **When you can't give customers what they are asking for, give them the next best thing!**

When customers communicate that they are upset because they can't get what they want, it is easy to respond defensively. Take the higher road instead. Listen for what the customers need and express that you are going to do everything in your power to help them resolve the problem.

Be proactive by focusing on what you can do to help the customer. If you need to involve someone else, take the initiative to seek the information or advice needed and return to the customer with a solution in hand. Doing this makes you the "service hero" in the customer's eyes.

"Don't worry about doing great things... just do little things with great heart!"

- Mother Teresa

Communicating with the Customer

Look at the differences in the statements listed in the two columns below. Which response would you prefer if you were the customer?

Avoid:	Replace with:
"I don't know."	"I'll find out."
"You want it by when?"	"I am going to get this to you as soon as I can."
"That's not my job."	"This is who can help you..."
"That's not my fault."	"Let's see what we can do about this."
"You need to talk to the manager."	"Let me see how I can help you."
"Calm down."	I am so sorry for your (inconvenience, disappointment, frustration).
"I'm busy right now."	"I'll be with you in just a moment (as soon as I done with this order.)
"Call back."	"I will call you back."

HOT TIP: Research shows that it takes six times more effort to attract a new customer than to keep a current one. Impress your employer by keeping your customer impressed with you!

3. **Surprise your customers by going beyond what is expected.**

In most cases, what it takes to shine in the eyes of customers is a simple sign of respect, a small gesture of kindness and consideration. Take the following examples:

- The gas station attendant who washes the windows of the customer in the self-serve lane.

- The dry cleaner who informs you, the customer, that she has replaced a button or two as part of the store's complimentary service.

- The receptionist who offers coffee to the client who has an extra long wait in the waiting room.

- The waitress who offers to divide a meal on separate plates for customers sharing one entrée.

- The store clerk who offers to draw a map for the customer to the place where she needs to go for a product his store does not carry.

*"I am only one;
but still I am one.
I cannot do everything,
but still I can do something.
I will not refuse
to do the something
I can do."*

- Helen Keller

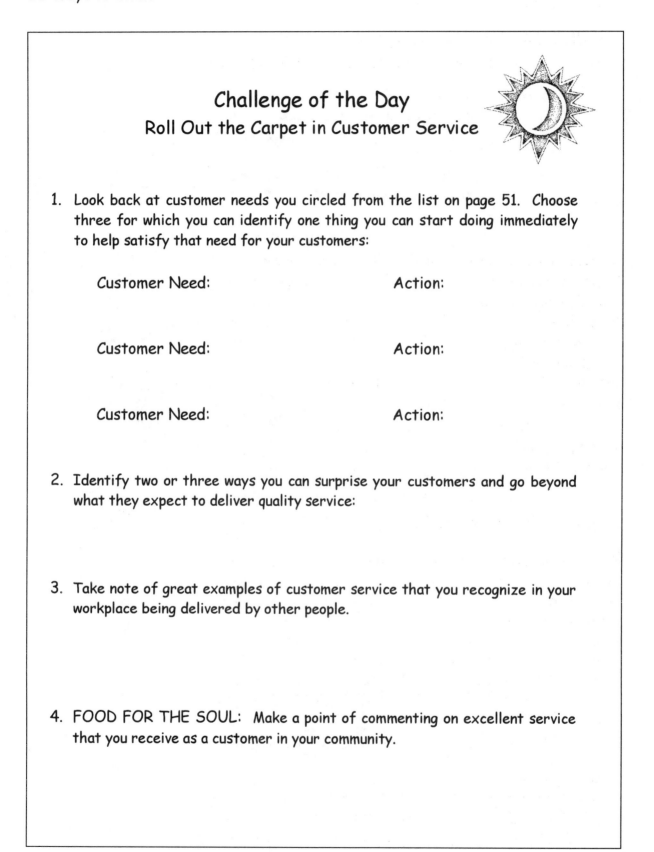

Challenge of the Day
Roll Out the Carpet in Customer Service

1. Look back at customer needs you circled from the list on page 51. Choose three for which you can identify one thing you can start doing immediately to help satisfy that need for your customers:

   Customer Need: Action:

   Customer Need: Action:

   Customer Need: Action:

2. Identify two or three ways you can surprise your customers and go beyond what they expect to deliver quality service:

3. Take note of great examples of customer service that you recognize in your workplace being delivered by other people.

4. FOOD FOR THE SOUL: Make a point of commenting on excellent service that you receive as a customer in your community.

SKILL 14: BEING A TEAM PLAYER
Develop Your Human Relations Skills

*"We get by with a little help
from our friends!"*

- The Beatles

By becoming a team player, not only do you get by with a little help from your newly-made friends, but you also become a more valuable employee! Did you know that employees who are good team players (helpful and easy to get along with) are valued more highly than people who have better technical skills but are hard to get along with? This is great news for you, because the ability to become a great team player is completely within your control!

HOT TIP: Increase your value as an employee by becoming a valuable player on the team!

Suggestions for Becoming a Great Team Player

Here are some simple suggestions for becoming a great team player! Place a check (✓) next to each suggestion you will begin to practice immediately. There are two items that will hinder, not help, your position on the team. See if you can spot the lemons.

1. ____ Once in a while, volunteer to do some of those tasks that get passed around because no one likes to do them.

2. ____ Tell co-workers when you hear something good about them.

3. ____ Tell co-workers when you hear something bad about them so that they can know what is being said and work to change it.

"We are each of us angels with only one wing. And we can only fly embracing each other."

— Luciano de Crescenzo

The test of thankfulness is not what you have to be thankful for, but whether anyone else has reason to be thankful that you are here.

4. ____ Treat every person (from the top to the bottom and everyone in between) with the same level of respect you would treat the company owner.

5. ____ Pass along information that you find valuable and think might benefit other people, technical or otherwise.

6. ____ Celebrate the differences between people. Look for what each person uniquely brings to the team. For each person, ask yourself, "What would our work team be missing if he/she was not here?"

7. ____ Praise co-workers for what they do well or for positive qualities you see in them. To make a compliment more meaningful, tell the person not just what you like or admire, but *why it is important*. For example, rather than simply state, "You are a very creative person," take it further by saying "I loved your idea this morning. It is something I never would have considered before." Or, after saying, "Thank you for being patient with me yesterday", add, "You made it a lot easier for me to learn the new program by not pressuring me."

8. ____ Pass on genuine praise about a co-worker to another person in your workplace. Develop the reputation of someone who supports and appreciates other people without an agenda.

9. ____ Look for situations where others' accomplishments and/or abilities are taken for granted. Find a process or system that is working very smoothly and acknowledge the people who are making it work. Make a point of championing one or more of your co-workers every week.

10. ____ Share credit for successes. For example, when someone praises you for a great day's work, say something like, "I couldn't have done it without Martha answering the phone!" This will mean a lot to Martha and will show your employer that you value teamwork.

11. ____ Look for big and little ways to impress people with your talents and personality.

12. ____ Learn what other people do so that you can appreciate their part on the team. A couple of good questions that people will like responding to are, "Would you mind telling me a little bit about what you do? What do you like most about your work? What is the biggest challenge you face?" Be sure to ask the person's permission to ask them some questions.

13. ____ Volunteer to help a co-worker with something they are having trouble with.

14. ____ When you are unsure about how to respond to a customer or how to proceed with a task, ask your co-workers what they would do in the same situation. Being asked for your opinion is flattering and it is a sign of respect. Just make sure you are asking at a time when it is convenient for them to respond.

15. ____ Learn to pronounce people's names correctly.

16. ____ When people share information about their family or their personal life, listen and remember what they tell you . . . it may be an invitation to friendship. Never pass on what has been shared with you in confidence, whether or not the person asks for your confidentiality.

17. ____ Pay attention to what is important to people - whether it's a new baby daughter, an electric car they are building in their garage or their beloved comic book collection. Asking about things that are important to people is one way of showing people that you listen and care about them.

"Help thy brother's boat across, and lo, thine own has reached the shore!"

\- Hindu Proverb

"It is beautiful about life that no man can sincerely try to help another without helping himself."

\- Ralph Waldo Emerson

The Lemons:

#3 As a rule, don't tell co-workers when you hear something bad about them – even when you think they should know. It puts you at risk for hurting their feelings and making them feel badly towards someone else or passing on what may have started as a nasty rumor. Instead, nip the negative comments in the bud the moment they come your way. Obviously there may be circumstances in which you have both the relationship and the information to justify going to the person and discussing what you heard – but proceed with caution.

#11 To be a great team player, it is much more important **to be impressed** with other people than to think about impressing them! People who try to impress others are usually perceived as being very self-centered and conceited. People who are impressed by others are perceived as being likeable and open!

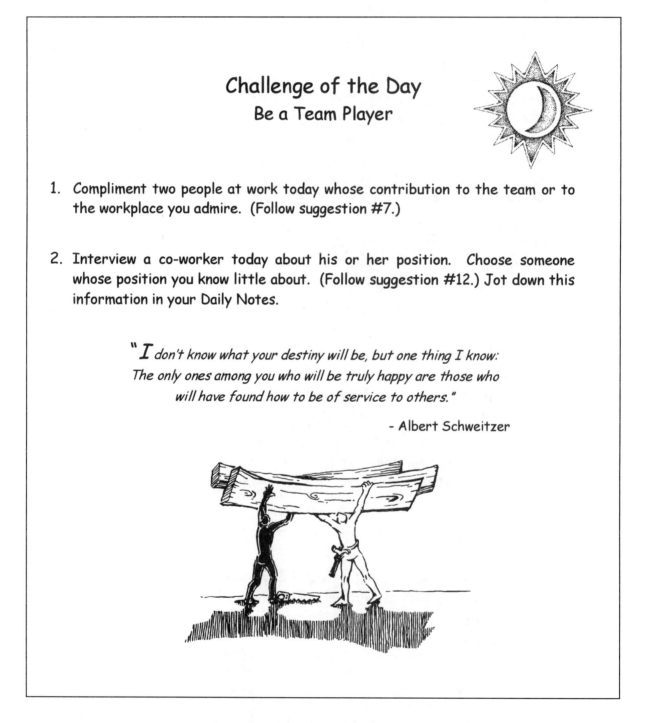

Challenge of the Day
Be a Team Player

1. Compliment two people at work today whose contribution to the team or to the workplace you admire. (Follow suggestion #7.)

2. Interview a co-worker today about his or her position. Choose someone whose position you know little about. (Follow suggestion #12.) Jot down this information in your Daily Notes.

"*I don't know what your destiny will be, but one thing I know: The only ones among you who will be truly happy are those who will have found how to be of service to others.*"

- Albert Schweitzer

SKILL 15: SURVIVING OFFICE POLITICS -
Develop Workplace Savvy

What is "Workplace Savvy"? It's understanding that getting along and succeeding on the job is not just about performing the job well, but relating well in a community of people. This is not always easy and it is not always simple due to the fact that most workplaces have what is called "office politics." Even if you can't escape office politics, it is worth considering what you can do to at least *survive* them! All but two of the following 21 items are HOT TIPS to follow while you are developing your workplace savvy. Two of these suggestions can get you into real trouble. Read through the list and see if you can spot them. Put a check next to those suggestions you plan to take seriously and put into use.

"You can hide from office politics but you can't escape them."

- Joan Fountain

HOT TIPS For Developing Workplace Savvy

1. _____ Company get-togethers are not the place to relax and say what you really think of the company health plan, your workload, or your boss's new haircut. Use good judgement inside and outside the company!

2. _____ Never complain about your boss to your co-workers or to someone in another department. Find a way to bring your complaint to your boss directly.

3. _____ Stay out of people's personal business and avoid fighting other people's battles.

4. _____ Accept that if your boss or supervisor thinks something is important, you should treat it like it is.

5. _____ Never pass on to other people what someone tells you in confidence - even if they didn't ask you to keep it secret.

6. _____ When others complain about a boss or co-worker, don't add fuel to the fire. It would be smarter to somehow change the subject.

7. _____ Don't take things - even little things - from work. It is stealing.

8. _____ Never ridicule anyone, even as a joke or to make a point, even if he or she laughs too. Avoid telling jokes or stories that could offend someone else, even if the person is not present. It could get back to them or offend someone who is present!

9. _____ Question authority, but question it to yourself until you have some authority.

10. _____ Know that what you say may not be what the other person hears, and what you hear may not be what the other person means. When you have a falling out with someone at work, check it out with the person so that misunderstandings can be cleared up.

11. _____ When people share their problems with you, give them advice based on what you would do if you were in the same situation.

12. _____ Say what you mean. Mean what you say. Do what you say you will do.

13. _____ Learn to say very little about things you know nothing about.

14. _____ Never assume it is okay to swear, even if others do.

15. _____ When you make a complaint, focus on the resolution you want to see rather than on the details of the situation that are bothering you.

16. _____ Never say anything at work you wouldn't want your boss and co-workers to hear.

17. _____ Take what people say about each other with a grain of salt. There will always be those who will try to color your thoughts and feelings about other people. Be your own judge of character.

18. _____ Avoid speaking when you are very upset. You can always decide to go back and say something to a boss or a co-worker later, but you can never *unsay* what you've already said.

*E*ngage brain before opening mouth.

19. _____ If you want to communicate something confidential or private to a co-worker, send an e-mail rather than saying it out loud where it can be overheard.

20. _____ Most of us have mastered the art of complaint in all its variations: gripe, groan, moan, whine and grovel. Don't pollute your work environment with complaints. Instead, ask yourself, "What would I like to have changed in this situation?" Suggesting the change will get you better results than spreading the complaint!

21. _____ If you believe you're a victim of sexual, racial, age or religious discrimination or abuse, tell your supervisor. If he or she is unwilling or unable to help, tell the next person up the line of command.

Where are the lemons?

#11: This suggestion could work some of the time, but most people don't want advice when they share their problems, they just want someone to listen and empathize or to agree that they're right. A good idea is to ask the person if he or she would like your advice before giving it.

#19: If you are concerned about privacy, don't put it in an e-mail! Employers are legally permitted complete access to your e-mail. (The courts so far have ruled that because the corporation owns the equipment over which the e-mail is sent, they also have access to its content.) If you think that hitting the delete key will solve the problem - think again. The file may disappear from your screen. But it does not disappear completely - it just moves to a delete folder. A good rule of thumb: Do not write an e-mail that you would not want showing up in the company newsletter!

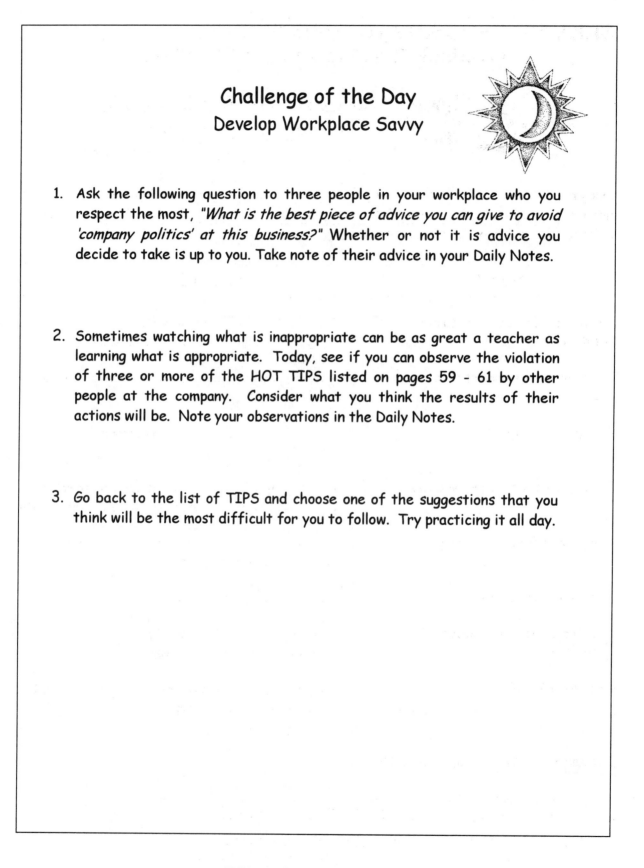

Challenge of the Day
Develop Workplace Savvy

1. Ask the following question to three people in your workplace who you respect the most, *"What is the best piece of advice you can give to avoid 'company politics' at this business?"* Whether or not it is advice you decide to take is up to you. Take note of their advice in your Daily Notes.

2. Sometimes watching what is inappropriate can be as great a teacher as learning what is appropriate. Today, see if you can observe the violation of three or more of the HOT TIPS listed on pages 59 - 61 by other people at the company. Consider what you think the results of their actions will be. Note your observations in the Daily Notes.

3. Go back to the list of TIPS and choose one of the suggestions that you think will be the most difficult for you to follow. Try practicing it all day.

SKILL 16: CHOOSING TO THINK POSITIVE
Overlook The Mud And See The Stars

*"Two men in prison looked through bars,
One saw mud, the other stars.*

- Langston Hughes

Imagine that we have two people working in the same job, experiencing the same things, and we get to read their minds! Read their thoughts and see if you can find a pattern of differences between the thoughts of Person A and Person B.

Person A	Person B
I have way too much work to ever get it all done!	I am going to work on the important things first and see what I can accomplish.
I'll never get the hang of this.	All I can do is my best. I am going to focus on the little piece in front of me.
This job is boring!	I am going to need to be very creative to enjoy this job.
These people are driving me crazy!	I control my own feelings. What can I do to not let the people around me disturb my own sense of peace?
I shouldn't have said anything.	Even though I didn't get the response I wanted, at least I spoke up for myself.
I just keep making mistakes!	I am learning a lot right now.
I've always had a hot temper, I can't help it.	I am bigger than my temper. I can respond in a more effective way.
I am so confused!	I've got a lot of questions I need answered before I am going to understand this.

Jot down the differences you notice:

Did you notice these differences in their thinking?

Person A's thoughts were:

Negative

- Based on powerlessness

- Focused on what was wrong with other people or in the situation

Person B's thought were:

Positive

- Based on his/her control in the situation

- Focused on what he/she could do to make the situation better

"Our best friends and our worst enemies are our thoughts."

- Gandhi

"The most powerful thing we can do to change our lives is to change how we think."

- William James

Is there any doubt as to which person is happier? Is there any question as to which person is more effective? I don't think so!

Here is the interesting part: they could be the thoughts of the same person! The thoughts on the left might be the *first thought* the person had, but because the mind is like a steering wheel that we can point in any direction, the thoughts on the right might be the *new thought* after a turning of the wheel!

For the most part we eat, work, worry, hope, plan, love, hate, shop . . . all with little attention to how we are thinking! We don't watch how the mind moves, what it fears, what it heeds, how it talks to itself, what it brushes aside. But the beginning of any positive personal change in our lives is incredibly simple: **We only have to pay attention to what we pay attention to!** Immediately we will have added a new perspective and that can change everything else! Where you once saw mud, you can see stars!

Ignore your thoughts and you are like a passenger strapped into an airplane seat, going where the mind wanders. Pay attention to your thoughts and you will be the pilot taking your mind where you want to go!

HOT TIP: Learn to steer your thoughts by becoming the pilot of your mind!

Challenge of the Day
Think Positive

1. List 5 things that are going right so far in this job:

   a.

   b.

   c.

   d.

   e.

2. The difference between an obstacle and an opportunity is how we think about it. List two obstacles or difficulties you are facing on the job and then write what opportunity you might find in that difficulty.

Obstacle	Opportunity
a.	
b.	

3. FOOD FOR THE SOUL: Spend some time in nature this week. Take a walk, go fishing, do some gardening . . . let nature nurture you and give you a fresh perspective.

SKILL 17: FACING YOUR FEARS AND FINDING COURAGE
Look The World Straight In The Eye!

"Never bend your head.
    Always hold it high.
        Look the world
            straight in the eye."
                - Helen Keller

Find me someone who is without fear and I will show you someone who has ceased to live. Fear is a part of life, it will always be with us in one form or another. The challenge is not getting rid of fear, but learning to live and act with faith and courage in the face of fear. Here are nine simple tips for facing your fears.

Nine Tips for Facing Your Fears

1. Accept fear as a companion in your life.

Accept the reality and presence of fear in your life. It's with us, it's part of us, whether we like it or not. To be completely fearless is to be either foolish or suicidal. Fear exists because life is scary and we prefer to feel safe. As long as we are alive, fear will be a faithful companion. Not always cheerful, sometimes annoying, but ever-present. Accept it, make friends with it – then give it as much power as you want it to play in your life - no more, no less.

2. Listen to what fear has to say.

Fear always has something important to say. It is a messenger. Whether we agree with that message or not depends upon what we *think* about it. Listen to it, then feel free to disagree. Ignoring fear makes it grow bigger and stronger. Listening to it makes it smaller. Take the advice of the great Vietnamese teacher, Thich Nhat Hanh, *"It is better not to say, 'Fear, I don't like you. You are not in me.' It is much more effective to say, 'Hello Fear. How are you today?' "*

3. Respect your fear.

Respect your fears. They are like a map that shows you where you've been and where you would just as soon not go again. You may not understand your fears, but they are yours, part of the treasure you have collected. They are as precious as gold because they were born of your experience. Even if others cannot understand and respect your fears, it is the least you can do for yourself!

4. Claim your courage!

Find comfort in the fact that where you feel fear, you can always bring your courage. Courage is as much in your nature as fear is and you have shown your courage time and again throughout your life. Stop and think about the last time you were truly courageous. (Probably when you accepted this job!)

"On you will go, onward up many frightening creek, though your arms may get sore and your sneakers may leak."

- Dr. Seuss

5. Think moment to moment.

You never need to muster enough courage to last a whole day or a whole week, much less a lifetime. What you need is the courage that gets you from one moment to the next moment. In the words of the spiritual teacher, Krishnamurti, "Life is a game of inches."

6. Learn to "do" courage.

Even when you don't feel particularly courageous or strong, fake it. Courage isn't always something we possess, sometimes courage is what we "do", no matter how we feel. If you were to "do courage" today, what would that mean? Since fear is just another kind of energy, is there a way you could use it as fuel for the fire?

"Every day has two handles. You can take the handle of hope and enthusiasm or the one of fear and anxiety. Upon your choice so will be your day."

- Unknown

7. Know what you can count on.

In the face of fear, it is important to stop and recognize everything in your life that you can count on. Seeing the parts of your life that are strong and where you can count on for some kind of comfort or support gives you courage!

8. Watch where you are putting your "faith".

Remember that we all have faith, all the time. The question is where we are putting it. Do you put more faith in your tendency to fail or your ability to overcome? When you feel afraid, a good question to ask yourself is, "What have I lost faith in? Have I lost faith in myself, in other people, in life, in God? Where do I need my faith restored?"

9. Stand by your heart!

The word courage actually comes from the French word "coeur", meaning "heart". Make a habit of standing by your heart! Like some people keep a gratitude journal, consider keeping a *courage journal*, noting at the end of every day how you mustered courage in big and little ways!

"What a new face courage puts on everything."

- Ralph Waldo Emerson

"The goal in life is not to get rid of the butterflies in your stomach, but to get them to fly in formation!"

- Outward Bound

Challenge of the Day
Facing Your Fears

1. Identify a few of your fears about your present work situation.

    Now consider for each:
    *   What is the worst case scenario?
    *   What is the best case scenario?
    *   What is the most probable scenario?
    *   What level of control do you have to affect the situation?

2. Confide in a mentor, co-worker or supervisor who you trust about these fears and get another perspective on the situation.

3. Everyone has their own brand of courage. You are never without its power! What does your courage look like at your present job? In relation to the fears you identified above, what is your courage asking from you? (For example, to speak up or to be silent, to show your power or to withhold it, to take a risk to try something new or to sit back and be patient?) Complete this sentence:

    I am showing my courage by:

4. In the light of whatever fear you are experiencing in your job or in your personal life right now, list below at least five important things you can count on in your life to see you through it. (For example, can you count on your friends or your family, your faith, your health, your sense of humor, your stubbornness, desire to succeed?)

    I can count on:

SKILL 18: BREAKING BAD HABITS OF THE MIND
An Experiment In Attitude

True or False?

T____ F ____ The things I expect to go wrong, usually do.
T____ F ____ The things I expect to go well, usually do.
T____ F ____ Most people treat me the way I expect to be treated.
T____ F ____ What I think about and talk about is what shows up in my life.
T____ F ____ Days that I expect to be wonderful before they begin
turn out to be so much better than the days I greet with grumbling.

If you answered the 5 statements above with "True", you agree with every psychologist in the world. The bottom line is "Attitude Matters!"

A Dozen Bad Habits of the Mind

We all know that attitude affects the quality of our everyday lives, so why do we have such a hard time keeping it in check? Probably for the same reason that most people know how to take care of their bodies, but don't. Simply put, bad habits are easier to keep than good ones. Here is a list of a dozen bad habits of the mind that affect our daily attitude. Put a check next to each one that you need to work on breaking:

____ Dwelling on the past
____ Holding grudges
____ Comparing yourself to others
____ Blaming other people
____ Always thinking the worst
____ Doubting yourself

____ Nursing old wounds
____ Noticing other people's faults
____ Feeling sorry for yourself
____ Coming up with excuses
____ Putting down your dreams
____ Doubting everyone else

So, how do we break those habits? By developing new ones! The mind can't straddle two lanes at the same time; it will either work on behalf of fear or of hope. It can't do both. So today put your mind to the test. Try an experiment with attitude. Don't worry, if you expect to prove us wrong, you will!

HOT TIP: Every day holds equal possibility for being wonderful because that possibility is in us and is something we *bring to* the day.

Challenge of the Day
Have a Positive Attitude

1. Instructions for an Experiment in Attitude:

    • Greet the day as if you expect it to be a good one.

    • Treat yourself as if you are the most important person in your life, that you matter to a lot of people and your time here is precious.

    • Notice the silent conversations you have with yourself. If they are negative, change the subject to something positive.

    • Ask what you can learn about yourself from people and situations that annoy you.

    • If you can, catch yourself in the act of any of the 12 bad habits of the mind and choose a new mode of thinking.

    • When you are frustrated, ask yourself if it will matter a year from now, and if not, take a deep breath and let it go.

2. Report your findings of this experiment in your Daily Notes. If you like what you learned, try doing this experiment for a whole week. Fair warning: repeated use of this experiment may result in you becoming a happy person!

3. FOOD FOR THE SOUL: Do something nice for someone in your personal life who could use a helping hand or an encouraging word.

SKILL 19: COPING WITH EVERYDAY LIFE:
The Art Of Flexibility

*"You can't stop the waves,
but you can learn to surf."*

- Anonymous

It has been said that real life is the collision - day in and day out - of the improbable with the impossible. How are you at coping with everyday life? To test yourself, consider how you would deal with the following situations:

- You misplace the keys to your car.
- You find your keys but your car won't start.
- Your phone gets disconnected because you forgot to pay the bill.
- You spill ketchup on your only clean uniform 10 minutes before work.
- Your computer crashes while you're working on an important document.
- You get a nice big glob of gum on the bottom of your shoes.

These situations probably sound familiar because real life is full of them, and now that you're in the work world, you're going to see a lot more of them. Successful people agree that happiness is not the absence of problems, but the ability to cope with them.

So how do you develop your ability to cope and be flexible? By coping and bending with what life hands you on a moment to moment, hour by hour and day by day basis. Every time we cope well with whatever life throws our way, we make a deposit in our self-esteem account. Make enough of those small deposits and pretty soon you are rich in flexibility and taking the roller coaster ride of life with your hands in the air!

"Have you ever noticed that life is not the way it is supposed to be? It's the way it is. So the way we cope with it is what makes the difference."

- Virginia Satir

HOT TIP: If there is one quality we need a lot of to deal with everyday life, it is Flexibility - the ability to go with the flow and not take anything too seriously. As the saying goes, "Blessed are the flexible, for they shall not get bent out of shape."

Challenge of the Day
Be Flexible

1. Observe yourself today and by the end of your shift, identify three areas of your work where you could expand your ability to be flexible and increase your ability to cope with the pressures of work. (Write about it in your Daily Notes.)

2. Observe the coping mechanisms of other people in your workplace today. Notice what seems to work for people and also notice what does not work.

3. Think about a person in your life who seems to really cope well - to take life's curves with finesse. What does this person do that enables that behavior? If you don't know, ask him/her.

4. If something happens today that upsets you, replace the tendency to say "Oh, shoot!" (or worse) with "Oh well!" It is amazing the difference you will feel with this change in your thought process!

5. Identify one aspect of your life where you place unnecessary stress on yourself and then begin to lay off. (Classic examples of ways of putting stress on ourselves include feeling you have to do everything perfectly, being overly concerned with some aspect of your physical appearance, or getting very bothered when plans change. What is your stress-inducing hang-up?)

SKILL 20 : TAKING SMALL STEPS TO CHANGE
Use Time Wisely

"It is when we make choices that we sit with the gods and design ourselves."

- Dorothy Gilman

How much time do you think you would need to truly accomplish all that you are capable of? To plumb the depths of your heart? To refine and parade your every talent? To stretch your imagination to its limit? To learn all that there is to know? To experience everything you want to experience? Would you need years? How about decades? Would you prefer an entire century?

Thomas Edison suggested that it would probably take *a thousand lifetimes* to accomplish all that we are capable of. But we don't have a thousand lifetimes; we just have one. And with that one we must settle to do the best we can with what we have. If we had an endless amount of time, there would be no need to set goals, plan carefully or choose direction. We could lay back, squander our time, and still manage to accomplish something wonderful. Time, however, plays a major role in our lives because we are never sure how much of it we have left. Because the clock never stops ticking, life asks that we pick a lane and choose a focus.

"True life is lived when tiny changes occur."

- Leo Tolstoy

Time is demanding, yes, but it is also amazingly fair and forgiving. No matter how much time we wasted in the past, we are always given a brand new tomorrow. If we spend one hour procrastinating, we are still given a fresh hour to start on priorities. One minute we can drift off and in the next moment we can concentrate completely.

Time is neutral – it passes regardless of how we spend it and it avails itself over and over again regardless of our plans. We need not worry about how to manage time because it is, by its very nature, unmanageable. What we can manage is how we use it!

HOT TIP: No matter what route you take, within 24 hours, your day will be over. Use it well! Don't think time management, think focus management.

Challenge of the Day
Make Small Changes

List two small changes you can make in the following areas to try this week.

Work Changes

Life Style Changes

Your exercise habits

1.

2.

Your eating habits

1.

2.

Use of your free time

1.

2.

Your home life

1.

2.

SKILL 21: CONTROLLING YOUR ANGER
Keep Your Head So You Don't Lose Your Job

Speak when you are angry
and you will make the best speech
you will ever regret!

"Anger is a signal, and one worth listening to."

\- Harriet Lerner

Anger. It's in the world. Always has been. Always will be. It's a universal experience that transcends time, cultures, and species. Dogs get angry. Bees get angry. And so does anyone who works. Anger is almost unavoidable in the day to day work world. That's the bad news.

The good news is that the disastrous effects that can come from an angry confrontation with a co-worker, customer or supervisor are avoidable! Here is a simple and straight-forward framework for handling anger on the job. Reading it now, while you are not in the throes of an angry moment, is good. Maybe some of these tips will help you when you're about to blow!

"Anger is loaded with information and energy."

\- Audre Lorde

5-STEP APPROACH
TO KEEPING YOUR HEAD AND YOUR JOB!

1. Read the signs!

Most people know when they are about to explode. There are usually physical signs that tell us we are about to lose it. Common signs include the face turning red, the heart pumping quickly, clenched teeth or tightened fists. The earlier you can get control, the better. Until you recognize and admit that you are angry, none of the other steps that follow will work.

What are your signs? What are your hot buttons? What is the earliest forewarning that should signal you to take a detour and head down a different road?

2. Take a time out.

This is the toughest part - having to keep your head so you don't lose your job. It is not unreasonable to request a short break or a few minutes to get control of your emotions. If you feel you are going to cry, throw a fit, yell, swear or in any other way "get physical" - take a break! Sometimes counting to 10 works - if you are really explosive, try counting to 100.

3. Figure out what you are angry about!

Identify the cause of your anger. Is it a broken down machine? An annoying customer? Harassment from a co-worker? Is it because your feelings are hurt or because you feel there is an unjust situation? Is it because you are not getting the recognition you feel you deserve or are you provoked by someone else's behavior?

Often the people we get upset with are not the true target of our anger, they just happen to be within range. It is important that you step back as an observer and ask yourself: What happened? What am I thinking? How am I feeling? How am I acting? The more you know about your anger and what caused it, the better you will be able to choose how to respond to it.

*"Anger is like milk,
It shouldn't be kept
too long."*

- Whoopi Goldberg

4. Get bigger than your anger!

Who is really the boss in your life? Your employer? I don't think so. Your highest values should be your guide - the part of you that acts on behalf of your highest good - from your deepest values. Empower yourself by acknowledging that you are choosing to keep your job. If you don't get bigger than your anger, the reaction that helps you release it may get you fired. Remind yourself that you (the one with a brain) are the one calling the shots here - not your hot-headed thoughts or hurt feelings. Take back the power that you may feel was taken from you and decide to handle your anger in a way that allows you to keep your job.

*"Anger makes us
look 10 years older
than we are, and at
the same time, like
a little child."*

- Maya Angelou

5. Choose your best response.

Choose your best response by asking yourself:

"Given the fact that I am angry and I want to keep my job, what can I do about it so that (1) I keep my job and (2) this doesn't happen again?"

Your options will probably include:

"Through anger, the truth looks so simple, but it is a curtain, not a window."

- Jane McCabe

- **Confront the person or situation that provoked your anger.**

  Can you do it without doing further damage to the relationship, your reputation or your position?

- **Do nothing at all.**

  See if when the smoke clears, it is a livable situation. Would doing nothing expose you to further conflict?

- **Make a complaint.**

  Is this a situation that should be brought to a third person in greater authority or knowledge who could bring about a change in the situation?

- **Seek advice.**

  Do you need support and advice from someone you trust before choosing your course of action?

- **Convert the anger into energy.**

"Anger makes us all look stupid."

- Nelson Mandela

  Anger is energy that can be worked to your advantage. Like an experienced swimmer, let the power of the current propel you. In this case, let the anger guide you upstream – to act productively. It's amazing what tasks you can accomplish while you are angry. Clean up your office. Work in your yard. Finish a long overdue report. Go for a swim.

Challenge of the Day
Control Your Anger

1. Identify the physical signs that tell you when you are about to blow:

2. Identify your hot buttons, things or situations that have set you off in the past that you should be aware of and avoid:

3. How do you usually react when you are angry? Do you yell or do you get silent? Do you cry or do you stomp your feet? Imagine yourself in your "anger mode" and consider whether or not your typical mode would be appropriate or acceptable in your workplace.

4. Write down the names of three people you could talk to for advice or support in a situation that was very upsetting.

5. Identify two or three tasks or activities you know you can do when you are angry.

6. Ask a mentor or supervisor who would be the appropriate person to go to if you were having a problem on the job.

SKILL 22: MAKING YOURSELF UNDERSTOOD
Choose The Right Words To Express Your Feelings

"Words are the most powerful drug of mankind. Choose them carefully."

- Rudyard Kipling

What's the difference between feeling unclear, confused, and totally baffled? How about the difference between feeling interested, energized and ecstatic? Even though the words in each sentence are similar in spirit, they take you to different places, don't they? Words can be enormously useful in helping us express our feelings, especially if they are chosen carefully.

Use this list of feeling words to develop your vocabulary for expressing your feelings. Notice that within each "feeling category", the words listed begin in the mild range and get stronger as you continue down the list.

Strength	Weakness	Excitement	Sadness
Adequate	Uncoordinated	Interested	Low
Able	Awkward	Attracted	Out of sorts
Capable	Ineffective	Enthusiastic	Disappointed
Effective	Incapable	Eager	Unhappy
Competent	Weak	Excited	Sad
Confident	Vulnerable	Fired up	Dispirited
Powerful	Helpless	Thrilled	Depressed
Dynamic	Unfit	Pumped	Anguished
Forceful	Powerless	High	Grieved

Fear	Confusion	Anger	Joy
Worried	Undecided	Irritated	Satisfied
Nervous	Unsure	Annoyed	Glad
On-edge	Vague	Put out	Good
Scared	Curious	Mad	Happy
Frightened	Confused	Frustrated	Cheerful
Apprehensive	Lost	Fed up	Up
Terrified	Perplexed	Furious	Elated
Panicky	Bewildered	Seething	Overjoyed
Desperate	Baffled	Enraged	Ecstatic

Challenge of the Day
Express Your Feelings

To practice identifying your feelings, use the list on the previous page to answer the following questions:

How did you feel when you were hired for this job?

How did you feel the first day on the job?

How do your feelings today differ from your feelings in the first week?

How did you feel the last time someone criticized your work?

How does it feel when you get the hang of a new part of your job?

How do you feel about answering questions about your feelings?

SKILL 23: BENEFITING FROM PRAISE AND CRITICISM
Respond Well To Feedback

Peer out the front window – glance out the back. Yesterday is past, tomorrow is the future. Today is the real gift. Good or bad, listen to feedback – learn from it, then let it go. You are a work in progress.

TIPS FOR RESPONDING TO FEEDBACK

When the feedback is positive:

1. Take a deep breath, smile, and say "Thank you".

   Don't let modesty or embarrassment keep you from accepting and receiving an honest compliment. Being able to take positive feedback gracefully is an important workplace skill: especially when you plan to shine with the skills you are learning through this guide! In fact, if you are afraid of positive feedback, you'd better stop reading now.

"This too shall pass."

Common knowledge

When the feedback is negative:

2. Deal only with the situation in front of you.

   Don't think how similar this is to another event or focus on a past experience that has caused you pain. Respond to this current situation rather than re-act (or acting again) to an old one!

3. Separate the facts of the situation from your feelings about it.

   Don't listen for details about what happened or didn't happen; listen for clues that lead to solutions! Take the difference between the following comments:

"But I did check in before 4:00!" vs. *"I know that you want me here on time."*

"Sue told me to do that!" vs. *"I need to listen to you even when I am being told something else."*

4. **Know that your version of the truth is not everyone else's verson.**

   Remember that everything you think is only your opinion, based on your experience. It is not the one and only truth. Someone may have a totally different understanding and you can both be "right".

5. **Remember that E+R = O.**

   An Event + your Response = the Outcome!

   When you are faced with the Event of negative feedback, think about the Outcome you most want in the situation, then choose the Response that will bring your desired result.

   For example, if someone falsely accuses you of stealing something, you can respond by blowing up and getting angry at your employer. This *aggressive* response will not necessarily bring out the truth of your innocence. You could respond in a *passive* way by not saying anything at all but that response carries the risk of the truth not coming out. An *assertive* response would entail approaching the manager very calmly and explaining that there has been a misunderstanding.

Tips 6-9 will help you to avoid aggressive and passive responses and to respond with assertiveness.

6. **Change your focus from "winning" to "agreeing".**

   Focus on solutions, what's next rather than dwelling on what went wrong. Support the idea that you can both win. Know that a disagreement is a clash of ideas, not persons.

Clarify what you absolutely need in this situation from what you want. The bottom line of compromise is what you need, not what you want. Come to an agreement that meets both your needs and the employer's needs so that you both win!

7. Cool off before responding.

If you feel that you have been treated unfairly, wait until after the heat of the moment to express yourself. You will communicate better when you are not feeling defensive. Simply listen to the criticism and ask for what they want to see in the future. Later, at the end of the day or the next morning, ask for a moment to talk with the supervisor or co-worker and begin by saying, "I'd like to talk about what happened yesterday."

Always resist the urge to yell at your boss, co-workers or customers, even if they yell at you. It's okay to ask for a break until you cool down. Take the high road.

8. Focus your time, energy and thoughts on areas where you have control.

You can't change the past, but you can affect the future. You can't always change someone else's mind, but you can change your own. Do something to help someone or engage in an activity that feeds your spirit. Keep busy; work out problems through physical activity. Concentrate on what is working in your life.

9. If you're going to fall, fall forwards.

Ask yourself what you learned. Take that lesson with you and use what you learned in the future. Don't waste your energy being angry with yourself. Sophocles said we're here to unravel the thread of life. Everyone comes into this life with a "full spool" that gets unraveled and raveled again. Remember, life's a spin. Don't obsess. Get on with it. Life's awaiting. Trust yourself not to make the same mistake. Be prepared to make a new mistake - a fresh one . . . that's how we learn.

"There are two rules in life... One, things never work out all the way. And two, they always turn around."

- James Webb

"The best way out is always through."

- Anonymous

Challenge of the Day
Respond Well to Feedback

1. Practice accepting positive feedback with a smile.

2. Think about the last time someone gave you negative feedback. How did you respond? Considering the tips listed, think about how you would respond differently in the future.

3. Invite constructive criticism by asking a supervisor or co-worker how you might improve in your work.

4. Keep the list updated in your Daily Notes.

SKILL 24: DEVELOPING THE ABILITY TO REALLY LISTEN
Be All Ears And Don't Tune Out

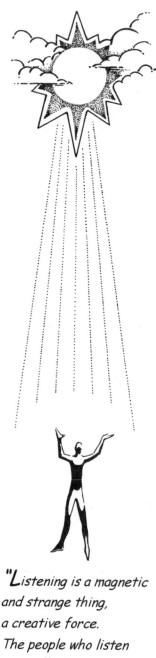

"Listening is a magnetic and strange thing, a creative force. The people who listen to us are the ones we move towards and we want to sit in their radius as though it did us good, like ultraviolet rays."
- Brenda Uleland

Please respond to the following statements by putting a check at True (T) or False (F).

T __ F __ 1. Most workplace errors happen not because of poor performance but because of breakdowns in communication.

T __ F __ 2. Listening is an activity that comes naturally - we all know how to listen.

T __ F __ 3. Listening and hearing are different things.

T __ F __ 4. Good communicators listen more than they talk.

T __ F __ 5. Good listening means focusing entirely on the words being spoken.

T __ F __ 6. What you hear is usually what was said.

1. TRUE. In fact, it is estimated that 70% of workplace errors happen because of communication breakdowns! Imagine the number of mistakes you can avoid just by developing the one key skill of listening!

2. FALSE. Contrary to popular belief, listening comes anything but naturally! Unlike breathing, listening is a mental process. You must first make a decision to listen, then use your good listening habits to do so. It is not a natural reflex, and as you may well know, certainly not everyone knows how to listen.

3. TRUE. Listening and hearing are different things. A person may hear well and also be a good listener or hear well and not be a good listener. Listening is about paying attention to what you hear. Think of all the things you do not hear in the course of a day that are within hearing range, but because your attention is elsewhere, the sounds don't register. (The humming of a computer, a birdsong out the window, the chatter of co-workers in the next cubicle, etc.) Listening is a filter in an expansive world of sound.

4. TRUE. Good communicators listen more than they talk. And not only are good listeners liked by everyone, after a while they know something! The behaviors of good communicators are not speaking, quoting and persuading - they are listening, asking questions, watching, evaluating, asking more questions, observing and learning! What easier way to stand out as a great communicator than to simply increase your ability to listen!

5. FALSE. Good listening does not mean focusing entirely on the words being spoken. Listening involves our ability to put together other kinds of information as well. It is estimated that only 7% of a message is formed by the actual words we choose. 38% of the message comes from **how** the words are spoken and 55% comes from non-verbal gestures, as in facial and body gestures, posture and eye contact. This is what is sometimes referred to as the "hidden dimension" of communication.

"We pretend that we use speech to express thought, but really it is the vehicle by which we express feeling."

- Henry David Thoreau

Experiment: Say the following sentence three times, each time applying a different meaning. Notice the changes in your body and voice as you change the meaning of the sentence.

This is a great place to work!

a. Say it meaning: I feel so lucky to work here!
b. Now, say it meaning: This is a terrible place to work!
c. Finally, say it meaning: You like to work here but you'd never come here as a customer!

What does this say about the importance of words?

---

6. False. What we hear is usually not what was said, but more a result of what we *expect* to hear, what we *want* to hear or what we *thought* we heard! Think about the last time someone misinterpreted what you said or you misunderstood someone else. Would the situation have been different if each of you had really listened to what was being said?

"It is a luxury to be understood."

- Ralph Waldo Emerson

HOT LISTENING TIPS:

- In the words of St. Francis, "Seek first to understand, then to be understood."

- Get out of your own way and shut off your own voice while people are talking;

- Listen for both the facts and the feelings behind what someone is saying;

- Comment on what you think the person is saying and ask if you are right; and,

- Identify your tune-out mode so you can notice and control it.

"When the eyes say one thing, and the tongue another, a practical man relies on the language of the first."

- Ralph Waldo Emerson

Identify Your Tune-out Mode

Here are six common and totally annoying non-listening behaviors. We all use these some of the time, even when we are not aware that we are tuning people out. Since the first step in controlling a bad habit is owning up to it, identify your preferred tune-out mode so you can catch yourself when you are in it and cut it out! Think about which mode you use with certain people at work. Check the one you want to avoid in the next couple of days. Come back to this list later to choose another to work on. If you don't know which one you use, ask your friend, a co-worker or a family member - they'll know for sure!

_____ The Daydreamer

Having a pleasant daydream? Catching a couple of ZZZ's? Thinking about your lunch hour or tonight's date? Have you ever looked in someone's eyes and realized they are off somewhere else? How did that feel? What did that mean to you?

_____ The Pretender

This is where you're on automatic pilot - you nod your head, smile in habitual mode and make noises like "uh-huh" . . . but you're not really there! When did you last fake your attention? Has anyone ever pretended to listen to you? Do you feel respected when people do that to you?

_____ The Fidgeter

If there's something on the table, you're playing with it. If there's a phone ringing, you're answering it. If there's music playing, you're tapping or humming or both. Worse yet, you may do all three at the same time! What do you find distracting when you are trying to listen to someone else? What do you do that others might find distracting?

_____ The Brick Wall

This is where you fold your arms and sit or stand as if you are the tallest person in the world - the message being, "Nothing you say is getting through to me! You might as well be talking to a brick wall!" When did you last do this? How were you feeling at the time? How do you feel when you're interacting with someone who is protecting him or herself from your words?

_____ The Politician

Have you ever talked to someone who just picked up on the points that were of interest to her and simply ignored the rest? Politicians, salespeople and mothers are famous for it. So are the rest of us when we ignore anything that leads to conflict, is difficult, embarrassing, bothersome or leads us to have to make a decision. Think about the last time you listened like a politician, selectively.   Did it help or hinder your relationship? How did it feel the last time someone did it to you?

_____ The Mindreader

This is when we interrupt people and finish their sentences. How does it feel when someone interrupts you? When have you played the mind-reader and been wrong?

"To truly be with people in conversation I think of myself, of my whole body, as an ear."

- Maya Angelou

"Maybe we were made with one mouth and two ears because we are supposed to do twice as much listening as talking!"

- Anonymous

Challenge of the Day
Practice Listening

1. Consciously practice the Hot Listening Tips all day today and see if you observe any differences in the quality of your interactions with other people.

2. See if you can catch yourself using one of the tune-out modes and refocus your attention. (Observe other people tuning you out. Ask them a direct question to refocus their attention.)

3. Ask someone a question you know they would love to answer and give them your full, undivided attention as they respond. Do this every day and you will be successful at developing a reputation as an excellent communicator!

4. Record in your Daily Notes what you learned about the power of listening from this activity.

SKILL 25: DEALING WITH DIFFICULT PEOPLE
Kill 'Em With Kindness

Entering the workplace brings with it the pro's and con's of participating in a new community. Certainly there is the joy of making new friends and learning from other people, but entering a new community also makes you vulnerable to criticism. Why? Because we human beings, in all of our imperfections, do not always treat each other kindly. In fact, sometimes we are downright rude, offering opinions or comments about things that are none of our business. After a while you learn to listen to other people's words and opinions with a kind of filter - you learn to take what will benefit you and leave the rest.

"No one can make you feel inferior without your consent."

- Eleanor Roosevelt

Words that are spoken with a positive intent are a gift - even when they are not always easy to hear. Words that are spoken with the intent to insult or hurt you are also a gift - but of a different kind. People who treat you disrespectfully provide you with the opportunity to hold to your own sense of worth and respect and not let them rock your boat! In other words, they are building your ability to sail smoothly even over rocky waves.

While this is not an easy skill to develop, it is an important one which will serve you well the rest of your life. Put a check (✓) next to each of the hot tips below that you can begin to practice immediately.

HOT TIPS
FOR NOT LETTING PEOPLE ROCK YOUR BOAT

1. ____ Don't wear the labels other people try to give you. If you feel belittled, neglected, ignored, ridiculed or rejected by someone at work, recognize this not as failure on your part, but as ignorance and lack of self-esteem on their part. People who need to belittle others obviously don't feel good about themselves.

2. ____ We know that misery loves company, but stay away from the pessimists and the complainers! It may feel like solidarity but it is actually climbing aboard a sinking ship. Surround yourself, instead, by people who are positive and enjoy their work. If you can't find anyone else who has a positive attitude, start the club and be its leader. There is nothing more contagious than happiness. It is difficult to remain neutral or negative in the presence of someone who is having a good time.

3. ____ When you feel harassed or poorly treated by anyone in the workplace, play the role of the "broken record" - communicate how you feel three times! Here are two examples. Note how the person is saying the same thing three different ways.

"Excuse me, but I did not appreciate that comment. Do not use words like that in front of me. Please do not treat me like that again." Or

"You really don't have to raise your voice with me. I care about what you have to say but I can hear it better if you are not yelling. Please don't scream at me again."

4. ____ When someone makes a rude comment, calmly say, *"Excuse me, what did you just say?"* or *"What did you mean by that?"* Give the person a chance to rethink.

5. ____ Find a way to make changes in yourself instead of someone else. Sometimes the results are the same.

6. ____ The art of being wise is the art of knowing what to overlook! Try to focus more on what someone might be needing in the situation than their sad way of asking for it. Don't judge people by their ugly moments. (Someone just may return the favor for you some day.)

7. ____ There is one additional tip for dealing with difficult people that deserves our attention and that is:

Kill 'em With Kindness!

The Power of Kindness

The great writer, Henry James, once said "Three things in human life are important: The first is to be kind. The second is to be kind. The third is to be kind." A more current writer, Wayne Dyer, shares similar advice when he said, "If you must choose between being right or being kind, always choose KIND."

It's fine advice, but can you imagine responding with kindness to any of the following situations?

- Someone criticizes you or your work in front of other people?

- Someone makes a rude remark or tells a joke at your expense?

- Someone makes fun of your appearance or your clothes?

- Someone blows up or blames you for something that you could not help?

"Forgive your enemies. It will drive them crazy."

- Martin Luther King,

Jr.

Why should you consider responding with kindness to situations of ignorance, cruelty or injustice? Well, there are three reasons.

1. Kindness might be your best option!

Well, I suppose you could fight fire with fire, but that could just as well escalate the situation, not make it better. (For example, insulting someone who has insulted you . . . or yelling back at someone who yells at you.) Why play a game that you find distasteful in the first place? You don't have to lower yourself to that level. Instead you can bring the person up to your level where kindness has more power than ignorance. (By the way, doesn't water work better at putting out a fire than more fire?)

"Taking an eye for an eye is a great way to blind the world".

- Dalai Lama

> "*B*e kind,
> for everyone you
> meet is fighting a
> hard battle."
>
> - Plato

2. **Sometimes kindness is exactly what the other person needs most.**

   Have you ever said or done something hurtful to someone not because they deserved it, but because they just happened to be in the path of your arrows? Often we are not the target of people's anger, but are within range. Give the person the benefit of the doubt that you were not the intended target. Who knows – their cat could have just died, their child might be in trouble at school, their mate might have just left town without so much as a note. We know that life is messy for everyone – maybe kindness is exactly what the other person most needs right now!

3. **Kindness works!**

   Even when it's not what the person needs or deserves, kindness works! By responding to conflict with kindness you will be practicing a strength and eliciting a power that is almost impossible to overcome. In the martial arts they talk about "keeping your center" - not letting people knock you off guard. Well, it is impossible to be "off center" and to be kind.

> "*M*y religion
> is very simple -
> My religion is
> kindness."
>
> - Dalai Lama

Challenge of the Day
Kill 'Em with Kindness

1. Think about the last time you openly criticized someone face to face or behind his or her back. Consider what it was you really needed and wanted from that interaction.

2. Observe the people in your workplace today and identify those who do not treat other people kindly. Without trying to analyze the person, make room in your mind for the idea that perhaps the person has low self-esteem and needs to look better by making other people look worse. Consider how you can help that person to feel better about him/herself. Take note of your observations in your Daily Notes.

3. Observe the people in your workplace who treat people well. Write in your Daily Notes some of their behaviors which you would like to excel in.

4. Begin building a community of positive people, one person at a time. Be its leader. Identify at least one person in your workplace who you enjoy being around and who treats other people well. Ask that person to join you for lunch or to have coffee.

5. Think of at least three ways to be kind to people in your workplace.

   a.

   b.

   c.

6. When you see a co-worker or a customer blowing up or being rude to someone else, offer to step in and "kill 'em with kindness". Sometimes it is easier to do this when you are not the target of the person's anger.

JOB SATISFACTION: SURVEY TWO

Please rate each statement from 1 to 4 using the following scale:
1 = Strongly Disagree   2 = Disagree   3 = Agree   4 = Strongly Agree

A: Performance Expectations and Workload

I know what is expected of me.	1 2 3 4
The priorities of my job are clear.	1 2 3 4
I know what I am doing right and what I am doing wrong.	1 2 3 4
I know what my supervisor thinks of my performance.	1 2 3 4
I know how to get the information I need to do my job	1 2 3 4
I have plenty to keep me busy at work.	1 2 3 4
This job is a good fit for my qualifications and skill-level.	1 2 3 4

B: Communication and Feedback

I don't have any problems with people here.	1 2 3 4
I feel able to communicate my needs and desires.	1 2 3 4
I know where to go when I have a problem.	1 2 3 4
I am not afraid of admitting when I make a mistake.	1 2 3 4
My supervisor gives me good feedback.	1 2 3 4

C: Teamwork and Belonging

I fit in here.	1 2 3 4
I work well with my co-workers.	1 2 3 4
I feel valued and respected here.	1 2 3 4
I feel like I am part of a real team.	1 2 3 4

D: Motivation and Personal Growth

My work is appreciated.	1 2 3 4
I am proud of what we do here.	1 2 3 4
I believe this job will help me progress in my vocational goals.	1 2 3 4
I enjoy my job and I like being at my workplace.	1 2 3 4
I am proud to tell people where I work and what I do.	1 2 3 4

E: Stress Management

I have enough time to do what I need to do at work.	1 2 3 4
I have confidence in myself to make the best of this situation.	1 2 3 4
I am able to make ends meet financially.	1 2 3 4
Personal problems are not interfering with my work life.	1 2 3 4
I have support systems in place to help me with personal issues.	1 2 3 4
I am taking good care of my health.	1 2 3 4

Date completed _____

"*Everybody can be great . . . because
anybody can serve. You don't have to
have a college degree to serve.
You don't have to make your
subject and verb agree to serve.
You only need a heart full of grace,
a soul generated by love.*"

- Martin Luther King, Jr.

SKILL 26: MAKING A DIFFERENCE
Focus On Your Purpose

There is a story about three stonemasons who were asked what they did for a living. The first one said with regret, "I am nothing but a stonemason . . . I lay stone all day!" The second one said with a smile, "I am a stonemason . . . I lay stone. But if you take a step back you can see that I am building a wall." The third one said, beaming with pride, "I am a stonemason . . . I lay stone. Of course, if you take a step back you will see that I am building a wall. But if you take another step back you will see that I am building a cathedral in this place!"

Which of the three stonemasons do you identify with the most - the one laying stone, the one building a wall, or the one building a cathedral?

Regardless of your response, I can guess which one you *want* to identify with most! As human beings we all want to feel that we are contributing to something bigger than ourselves! Luckily, we all have the power to build cathedrals wherever we are, in every line of work! Take the following examples:

"Give me a place to stand and I can move the world."

- Archimedes

- The office clerk who works for a doctor and knows that he is affecting the health care of hundreds of men, women and children!

- The food service worker who figures that everyone deserves a wonderful dining experience, even in a school cafeteria!

"We make a living by what we get, we make a life by what we give."

- Sir Winston Churchill

- The auto-assembly worker whose work is inspired by the realization that each car will be taking a family safely on their many journeys.

- The child care worker who knows that she is making it possible for ten parents to go out and make a living because their children are in her care.

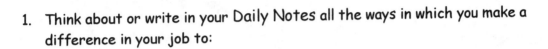

Challenge of the Day
Make a Difference

1. Think about or write in your Daily Notes all the ways in which you make a difference in your job to:

   • Clients and customers

   • Co-workers

   • Management

   • Others:

2. It is said that, "To the same degree as you are helpful, you will be happy." Put it to the test. Think of as many ways as you can to practice generosity today.

   For example, share your ideas, smiles, compliments, your bottled water, your life savers, your gum, a ride home for someone, an extra helping of patience for a customer. Knock yourself out with generosity and I'll make you a bet – it will be one of the best days you've ever had at work!

Nothing you ever do will be meaningless,
because the meaning is in you.
No task is without purpose.
Life is for giving, not getting.

SKILL 27: TAKE THIS JOB AND LOVE IT
Put Your Values To Work

> **HOT TIP:** Joy, purpose and belonging don't come with the job like tools or a uniform - they are qualities you *bring to* the job! We must be true to the qualities that support what we value!

Identifying Your Work Values

Listed below are twelve Work Values, benefits that you gain from working. Here is an opportunity for you to think about the Work Values that matter most to you. For each of the items, check column "A", "B" or "C" according to how important it is in your work at this time in your life.

A - Not very important   B - Would be nice to have   C - Very important

A   B   C

____ ____ ____ Enjoyment (Having fun at what you do.)

____ ____ ____ Purpose (Helping other people.)

____ ____ ____ Community (Making friends with co-workers.)

____ ____ ____ Freedom (Having flexibility and independence on the job)

____ ____ ____ Recognition (Being recognized for your work)

____ ____ ____ Creativity (Expressing yourself and your talents at work)

____ ____ ____ Achievement (Having a sense of accomplishment)

____ ____ ____ Variety (Having a mix of tasks to perform)

____ ____ ____ Security (Feeling a sense of stability)

____ ____ ____ Importance (Being seen by others as successful)

____ ____ ____ Aesthetics (Beauty of your work environment)

____ ____ ____ Growth (Learning and growing new skills)

Now, think about your current job. How many of the values you have marked "C" for "very important" are being fulfilled through that job? In each of those areas, ask yourself the following questions:

- What can I do to bring more of that quality to my job?

- How can I bring more of this into my life *outside* my job?

- As I consider future employment opportunities, what questions can I ask before, during and after the interview to better screen and choose a work environment that is true to my values?

Find a happy person and you will find her doing happy things. Find a person who values "achievement" and you will find a person busy achieving. It's time to make a habit of your values!

Challenge of the Day
Put Your Top 3 Values To Work

Choose your top three Work Values from the list of twelve and write them in the space below. Under each item, write two small steps you can take or things you can do to bring more of that quality to your present work situation. (For example, if you value Community, you can make a point of having lunch with different people throughout the week. If you value Aesthetics, you can decorate your personal work space. If you value Growth, you can seek advice from a mentor or supervisor on a class you should take outside of work to grow your skills.)

1. Top Value:
   One step I can take today/this week:

2. Top Value:
   One step I can take today/this week:

3. Top Value:
   One step I can take today/this week:

SKILL 28: LIVING EACH DAY GRATEFULLY
Redefine Wealth

THE SCULPTOR

I woke up early today, excited over all I get to do before the clock strikes midnight. I have responsibilities to fulfill today. I am important. My job is to choose what kind of day I am going to have.

Today I can complain because the weather is rainy, or . . .
I can be thankful that the grass is getting watered for free.

Today I can feel sad that I don't have more money, or . . .
I can be glad that my finances encourage me to plan my purchases wisely and guide me away from waste.

Today I can grumble about my health or . . .
I can rejoice that I am alive.

Today I can lament over all that my parents didn't give when I was growing up, or . . .
I can feel grateful that they allowed me to be born.

Today, I can cry because roses have thorns, or . . .
I can celebrate that thorns have roses.

Today I can mourn my lack of friends, or . . .
I can excitedly embark upon a quest to discover new relationships.

Today, I can whine because I have to go to work, or . . .
I can shout for joy because I have a job to do.

Today, I can complain because I have to go to school, or . . .
Eagerly open my mind and fill it with rich new tidbits of knowledge.

Today stretches ahead of me, waiting to be shaped.
And here I am, the sculptor who gets to do the shaping.
What today will be like is up to me. I get to choose what kind of day I will have!

Have a GREAT DAY. . . unless you have other plans.

A copy of "The Sculptor" came to me anonymously over the net. I know two things about the person who wrote it without needing to meet him or her:

(1)   This is a person who lives gratefully and who enjoys great wealth, regardless of his or her financial situation; and,

(2)   This is a person who has an attitude of gratitude, and because of it, loves his or her life!

We were not put on this earth simply to make money and ignore everything else. After all, Jesus never reached his income potential and the Buddha gave up all of his worldly goods. We come into this world with nothing and we take nothing with us when we leave. If there is any truth in the bumper sticker, "Whoever has the most toys wins!", my question is, what are we playing?

Here are three simple but powerful suggestions that if practiced daily can bring you a renewed sense of abundance and wealth:

1. Expand your definition of wealth!

Thinking of money as the only form of wealth is foolish. Check (✓) the items from the list below that you would include in your definition of wealth.

____ Good health   ____ Talent and skills

____ Education   ____ People who love me

____ A regular paycheck   ____ People I care about

____ Time for myself   ____ Freedom to make choices

____ Time to play   ____ Time to be of service to others

____ Time for my family   ____ Independence

____ Time with friends   ____ Good relationships

____ A roof over my head ____ Food on my table

How many of the things you checked from the list above are things you could not buy even if you wanted to?

"He who is not contented with what he has would not be contented with what he would like to have."

- Socrates

"To know when you have enough is to be rich."

- Lao-tzu

What if you were to measure your wealth, not by the things you have, but by the things you have that you would not exchange for money? Would you sell your eyes for a million dollars . . . or your two legs . . . or your hands . . . or your hearing? How much would you sell your friendships for . . . your family ties? Add up what you have in your life right now for which you would take no money, and you will find just how incredibly wealthy you already are!

> HOT TIP: Happiness is not a result of getting what you want, but wanting what you already have. If you aren't happy now, what makes you think you will be happy with more?

If you want to know how rich you really are, find out what would be left of you tomorrow if you should lose every dollar you own.

2. Make GRATITUDE a daily practice.

We always expect that happy people are grateful - but the opposite is even truer - it is grateful people who are happy! Meister Eckhart once said, if "thank you" were your only prayer, it would be enough. It seems that gratitude is not only the greatest of virtues, but the one that all the rest stem from! Every religion throughout time has espoused a common thread - count your blessings. Set aside time each day . . . when you awaken in the morning, at mealtimes, before bed, to make a practice of Gratitude.

> HOT TIP: Every life has its dark and cheerful hours. Happiness comes from choosing which to remember.

I cried because I had no shoes until I saw a man who had no feet.

- Persian saying

3. Take the time to marvel at the wonders of your life.

Sarah Ban Breathnach in her powerful book *Simple Abundance* asks a very profound question, "What if we were accountable for every permissible thing we might have enjoyed in life but did not?" The thought gives you pause, doesn't it?

Human beings have an almost infinite capacity for taking things for granted. Big things, like health or family. Little things, like the smell of rain or shadows around the moon. But as Henry Miller noted, "The moment one gives closer attention to anything, even a blade of grass, it becomes a mysterious, awesome, indescribably magnificent world in itself." Or in the words of Ralph Waldo Emerson," If the stars should appear but one night every thousand years how man would marvel and adore." But does the fact that the stars come out each night take away from their brilliance, from the miracle of their twinkling? Only if we let it.

E.B. White once stated, "Every morning I wake up torn between a desire to save the world and an inclination to savor it. This makes the day hard to plan." If we forget to savor the world, what possible reason do we have for saving it? In a way, our ability to marvel at the wonder of the world must precede our work to improve it, to add to it, or to change it.

> "*C*elebrate your existence!"
>
> - William Blake

> "*I*f you can walk you can dance. If you can talk you can sing."
>
> - Zimbabwe proverb

HOT TIP: Practice loving your life and your love for work will grow!

> "*B*e happy. It's one way of being wise."
>
> - Colette

Challenge of the Day
Practice Gratitude

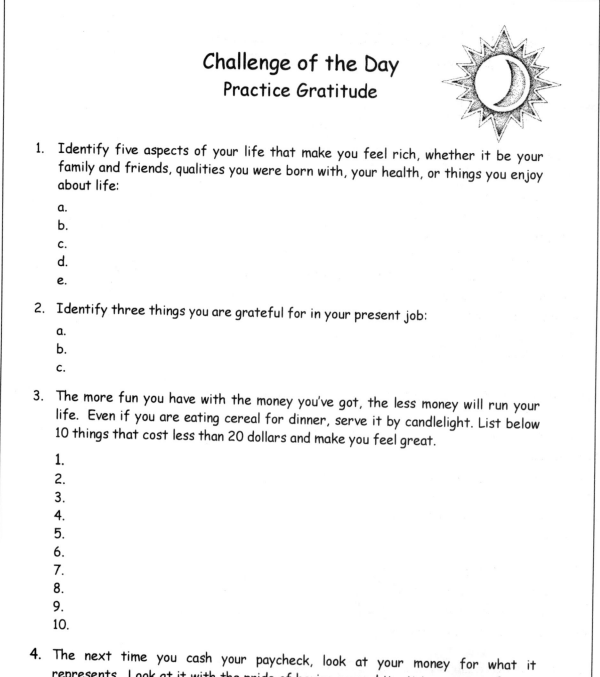

1. Identify five aspects of your life that make you feel rich, whether it be your family and friends, qualities you were born with, your health, or things you enjoy about life:

   a.

   b.

   c.

   d.

   e.

2. Identify three things you are grateful for in your present job:

   a.

   b.

   c.

3. The more fun you have with the money you've got, the less money will run your life. Even if you are eating cereal for dinner, serve it by candlelight. List below 10 things that cost less than 20 dollars and make you feel great.

   1.

   2.

   3.

   4.

   5.

   6.

   7.

   8.

   9.

   10.

4. The next time you cash your paycheck, look at your money for what it represents. Look at it with the pride of having earned it - it is one sign of a job well done. It is also a sign of the community to which you belong. Part of what you earned goes to taxes with which highways are paved, health care is provided and teachers are paid. Some of it goes into Social Security and helps pay the living expenses of the elderly. Being proud of your money and what you did to earn it may help to remind you to spend it wisely.

SKILL 29: LEARNING FROM A MENTOR
A Smart Step In Moving Forward

Asking for Help – A Parable

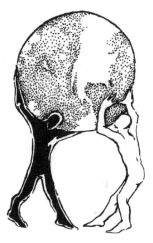

Once upon a time a boy and his father were walking along a road when they came across a large stone. The boy said to his father, "Do you think if I use all my strength, I can move this rock?" His father answered, "If you use all your strength, I am sure you can do it." The boy began to push the rock. Exerting himself as much as he could, he pushed and pushed. The rock did not move. Discouraged, he said to his father, "You were wrong. I can't do it." His father placed his arm around the boy's shoulder and said, "No, son. You didn't use all your strength . . . you didn't ask me to help."

Introduction to Mentoring

What does that little story have to do with career development, you ask? Everything! No one got to where they are without asking for help, not just once, but time and time again. The more comfortable you get with asking for help, advice and support the better! This practice is called "mentoring".

Not only is that a common practice in business, it is a highly valued practice! Many companies set up formal "mentoring programs" to ensure that all of their employees are getting the support and advice they need to grow.

There are three reasons you should consider seeking a mentor:

1. It is flattering to be asked for advice or support. It is a way of showing people that you respect them and want to learn from them.

2. Your willingness to ask for help shows a few things: initiative, confidence and humility.

3. It is simply a smart career move!

Common Questions about Mentorship

Where did the concept of mentorship come from?

"Do all the good you can
By all the means you can
In all the ways you can
At all the times you can
To all the people you can
As long as ever you can."

- John Wesley

Some people believe that the concept of mentoring was born out of the need for modern day companies to establish better ways for their employees to network. But that is not true. In fact, mentoring is not a modern day concept. The term "mentor" actually originated in classic Greek mythology. King Odysseus asked his friend, Mentor, a wise teacher, to watch over his beloved son, Telemachus, as the king embarked on an extended journey. As a substitute parent, Mentor offered support, guidance, protection and blessing to the young child until his father returned. It is from this classic example that we have come to know "mentors" as those who guide and nurture the growth of others through various stages of their development. Mentoring occurs between individuals, entities, organizations and nations. In fact, whenever two or more gather in the name of support and wisdom, there is mentoring.

What kind of help or support does a mentor give?

It totally depends on what you need and want. Here is a list of six different kinds of help or support you can request from a mentor:

1. Support and encouragement as you continue learning

2. On-going informal feedback to let you know how you are doing

3. Someone to go to when you have a problem or a question

4. Visibility or exposure to other people you should meet

5. Information on an event or a meeting you should attend

6. Participation on a task or an assignment whereby you will receive:

   • Valuable experience

   • Development of a new skill

   • Career advice

Just remember - a mentor is not expected to be all things! Typically, you would ask a person for help or support in one of the areas listed, not all of them!

What kind of time goes into a mentorship?

A mentoring relationship may require as little as 10 minutes a week for 3 or 4 weeks or as much as a lunch hour a week for a year. The two people involved decide among themselves how often they will meet and for how long. The timelines may change as the relationship changes. It is in constant negotiation. Some mentoring relationships last a week or a month while others continue for many years. Like any other relationship, it is difficult to predict because it evolves in its own time. A good rule of thumb is to ask the mentor how much time he or she has available.

What kind of position should a person be in to become a mentor?

The mentor's position or level in the organization is irrelevant. You should choose a mentor based on values, experience, interests and knowledge. Perhaps you will ask the receptionist for some communication tips and feedback on your interpersonal skills while you go to the Human Resource Manager for career advice. Go to the person who you think can help you most, regardless of position. (Think about someone you could mentor in one of the areas listed above!)

How many mentors can you have at one time?

Obviously, we are using the term "mentor" loosely here, but there is no limit to the number of mentoring relationships you can be involved with at any one time except in the limits of your time and energy. As a new employee, you might have a mentor assigned by your company who answers questions and helps you become acclimated to the workplace. At the same time, you may be going to a co-worker for some advice on meeting people and to a job counselor for ideas on upgrading your computer skills at night.

"If you can't run, walk. If you can't walk, crawl. But by all means, keep moving."

- Martin Luther King Jr.

How do I approach people to ask for help?

The straightforward approach usually works well. For example,

"A sure way for one to lift himself up is by helping to lift someone else."
— Booker T. Washington

"Hey, Sam, do you think you could spare a few minutes now and then to give me some feedback on how I am doing?"

"Susan, I am so impressed with your sign language skills. I would really like to learn some signs so that I can communicate with some of our deaf customers. Would you be willing to teach me a sign a day?"

"Mr. Huynh, could I buy you a cup of coffee sometime and get your opinion on a career plan I am working on?"

If it makes you more comfortable, use the Mentoring Checklist on the next page.

Challenge of the Day
Seek a Mentor

1. List three people from whom you will seek advice on mentoring opportunities.

   a.

   b.

   c.

2. Use the Mentoring Checklist to gather ideas from people listed above on on-going mentoring.

Mentoring Checklist

In today's world of work, it is important to continually learn and develop one's skills and network. To this end, I am seeking counsel and advice. Can you assist me in any of the following ways or refer me to someone else who can? Any ideas you might have would be appreciated. Thank you!

My present position is:

My vocational goal is:

_____ Visibility or exposure to other people I should meet:

_____ Information on an event or a meeting I should attend:

_____ Participation on a project or an assignment that will give me increased exposure and experience:

_____ Development of a new skill:

_____ On-going informal feedback:

_____ Support and encouragement as I continue learning:

_____ Career advice:

Ideas:

Other people I should talk to:

SKILL #30: BALANCING LIFE AND WORK
Food For The Soul

It has been said that there are three ways to change your life:

(1)   Keep doing what works.

(2)   Stop doing what doesn't.

(3)   Start doing what will.

So far this little guide has provided you with 29 skills that you can start using to improve your work life. This one falls last, not because it is least important, but because I want this guide to end with what may be the most important skill: to bring balance to your life and work.

Oddly enough, this is a skill that takes tremendous attention and discipline to develop. If you need any proof, look around in your community at what may be the majority of employed people who feel over-worked and under-lived. In other words, they feel as if they are "being worked" instead of working, dying rather than living. All other life on the planet has the intelligence built into it to balance work with play, activity with rest, dark with light, night with day. Only human beings attempt to live in a one-sided manner and it obviously doesn't work because it goes against our very nature.

Five Reasons to Create a Balance
Between Your Life and Work

The purpose of this skill is to develop an attitude and a stance towards your job so that it is only one part of your life, albeit an important part, but not necessarily the *most* important part. Before you have me arrested for treason by the Employer Police, hear me out. Here are five reasons why creating balance in your life will work for your career, not against it.

Do what you love, even if as a hobby!

1. Employees who are happy in their work are generally those who are happy in their lives, and vice versa.

    Contrary to popular opinion, it is not the over-achieving employee who lives to work who enjoys the most career success. That's the person who burns out or later down the road regrets all of the other aspects of life he or she sacrificed in the name of "work". You know it is true – no one on their deathbed ever wished they had put more time in at the office.

2. Employees who are physically active and enjoy a creative outlet come to work stimulated and energetic.

Put some money in a savings account every payday!

3. Employees who are connected with friends, family and/or other community groups bring a richness and diversity of human relation skills.

4. Employees who balance life and work will be best prepared to deal with the inevitable twists and turns in the 21st century work world.

    Why? Because it is people who have healthy physical, social, family and spiritual lives who find themselves with the confidence and support to take risks, to deal with change and to seek new opportunities – three important career strategies!

5. A balanced life is a way to prevent and deal with stress!

    Believe it or not, this is the skill for Stress Management. I didn't call it that because I think it is more an issue of managing your goals, your expectations, your time and your choices than it is of managing stress. Stress is just energy that gets blocked or built up. Energy is wonderful . . . it is the stuff of life! Knowing how to work with it is the trick. This guide is full to the brim with ideas on how to focus your time and energy at work. In the cultivation of this last skill, I want you to consciously give attention to focusing your time and energy on other parts of your life.

    This Challenge of the Day is one that you will go back to time and again because it contains so many ideas and it will probably get you thinking of many of your own. Take the following assessment in order to make your choices for Food for the Soul.

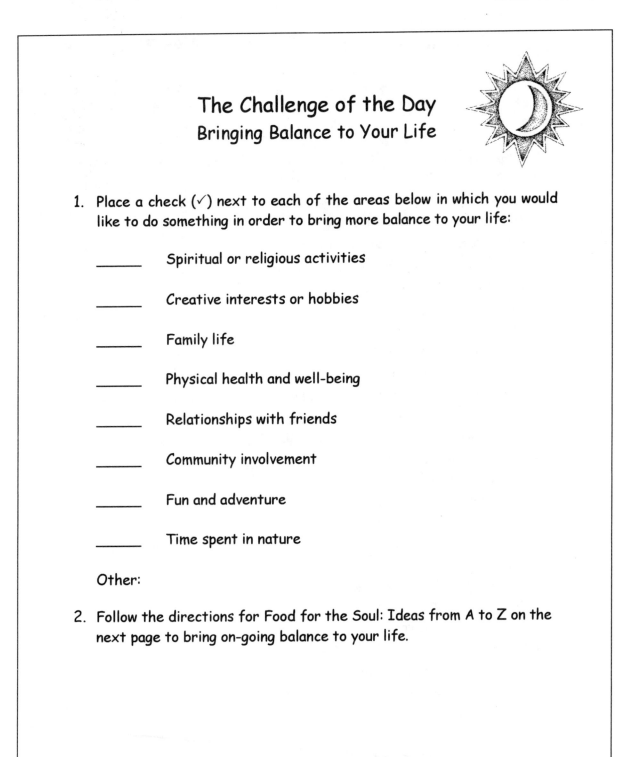

The Challenge of the Day
Bringing Balance to Your Life

1. Place a check (✓) next to each of the areas below in which you would like to do something in order to bring more balance to your life:

   _____ Spiritual or religious activities

   _____ Creative interests or hobbies

   _____ Family life

   _____ Physical health and well-being

   _____ Relationships with friends

   _____ Community involvement

   _____ Fun and adventure

   _____ Time spent in nature

   Other:

2. Follow the directions for Food for the Soul: Ideas from A to Z on the next page to bring on-going balance to your life.

Food for the Soul: Ideas from A to Z!

Listed below are 26 suggestions for feeding your spirit in simple ways outside the job. Place a check (✓) next to each of the suggestions you would consider trying. Choose three of these ideas to put into action immediately.

a. _____ Take up an artistic hobby like watercoloring, juggling or using computerized graphics to make greeting cards. Expand your creative horizons!

b. _____ Find a way to make each person in your home feel appreciated.

c. _____ Go for a hike somewhere in nature.

d. _____ Volunteer to read to children in a hospital.

e. _____ Turn off the T.V. an hour earlier than usual and read a book.

f. _____ Donate blood to a blood bank.

g. _____ Call and offer a sister, your mother, a neighbor or your child's teacher "two hours on Saturday morning" to use as they wish.

h. _____ Tend a garden or simply plant seeds in a small pot.

i. _____ Make a gesture of peace to someone in your life where it is needed.

j. _____ Ask a question of an elderly person that he or she would love to answer.

k. _____ Give a small child your total and undivided attention for a sustained period of time.

l. _____ Write to someone you admire and tell him or her why you feel that way.

m. _____ Celebrate a small event in someone's life in a big way! (For example, the purchase of a new car, a lost baby tooth, or getting hired at a new job.)

n. _____ When in doubt, give the right of way to the other driver at every stop sign. Practice kinder and gentler driving habits!

o. _____ Host a party for friends and have everyone bring a favorite piece of music, poem or artwork.

p. _____ Cook a gourmet meal for your family.

q. _____ Memorize your favorite poem.

r. _____ Volunteer at a soup kitchen. Serve it up with love!

s. _____ Go somewhere you've never been before.

t. _____ Redecorate a room in your house.

u. _____ Make a gift for someone special in your life.

v. _____ Call or write to a person in your life you care a lot about but haven't had contact with in a long time.

w. _____ Learn to play a musical instrument.

x. _____ Organize a donation for a family that needs help.

y. _____ Clean out your closets and give the things you are not using to a local charity.

z. _____ Write a speech that begins with the words, "I have a dream . . . "

JOB SATISFACTION: SURVEY THREE

Please rate each statement from 1 to 4 using the following scale:
1 = Strongly Disagree   2 = Disagree   3 = Agree   4 = Strongly Agree

A: Performance Expectations and Workload

I know what is expected of me.	1 2 3 4
The priorities of my job are clear.	1 2 3 4
I know what I am doing right and what I am doing wrong.	1 2 3 4
I know what my supervisor thinks of my performance.	1 2 3 4
I know how to get the information I need to do my job	1 2 3 4
I have plenty to keep me busy at work.	1 2 3 4
This job is a good fit for my qualifications and skill-level.	1 2 3 4

B: Communication and Feedback

I don't have any problems with people here.	1 2 3 4
I feel able to communicate my needs and desires.	1 2 3 4
I know where to go when I have a problem.	1 2 3 4
I am not afraid of admitting when I make a mistake.	1 2 3 4
My supervisor gives me good feedback.	1 2 3 4

C: Teamwork and Belonging

I fit in here.	1 2 3 4
I work well with my co-workers.	1 2 3 4
I feel valued and respected here.	1 2 3 4
I feel like I am part of a real team.	1 2 3 4

D: Motivation and Personal Growth

My work is appreciated.	1 2 3 4
I am proud of what we do here.	1 2 3 4
I believe this job will help me progress in my vocational goals.	1 2 3 4
I enjoy my job and I like being at my workplace.	1 2 3 4
I am proud to tell people where I work and what I do.	1 2 3 4

E: Stress Management

I have enough time to do what I need to do at work.	1 2 3 4
I have confidence in myself to make the best of this situation.	1 2 3 4
I am able to make ends meet financially.	1 2 3 4
Personal problems are not interfering with my work life.	1 2 3 4
I have support systems in place to help me with personal issues.	1 2 3 4
I am taking good care of my health.	1 2 3 4

Date completed _____

EPILOGUE
Keeping A Foot In The Future - Cultivating True Livelihood

"Luck is that place on the road where opportunity and preparation meet!"

"All glory comes from daring to begin."

— Anonymous

The rules of the workplace have undergone tremendous change and with them, so have the rules for career success. Here are some important suggestions for cultivating a livelihood that is true to your needs, interests and talents while being responsive to new realities of the 21st century work world!

1. Know Yourself.

Never has the need to know yourself, your values, motives, and desires, been more important for career success than in today's self-driven market. You need to have your finger on the pulse of your assets and your strengths, as well as your weaknesses as perceived from the employer's point of view. You also need to be able to communicate your strongest selling points to your market.

2. Keep Adding to Your Personal Toolkit.

It is common knowledge today that the only kind of job security worth pursuing is the security that comes from the *marketability* of your skills and continually adding value to your workplace. With constantly changing work and shifting skill requirements, "lifelong learning" is more than just a catch phrase; it is a necessity. Do whatever is necessary on your own time to ensure the currency of your skills. Continually ask yourself questions like:

✓ Am I feeling stretched in a positive way?

✓ What have I learned in the last six weeks?

✓ What do I hope to learn in the next six weeks? How about in the next six months?

3. Prepare for Skill Areas, Not Jobs.

It does not make sense to prepare yourself for future jobs and job titles that could change or vanish in a blink. Instead, focus on developing skill areas that are likely to be in demand in the future. Be flexible and adaptable and ready to try new ways of working, even if those ways of working are initially uncomfortable for you or different from what you are used to.

✓ Can you think of two or three skills that you perform in your current position which are transferable to other positions?

✓ Can you identify two or three skills that you use outside your particular job that you could transfer to another work setting?

✓ Do you know what skills and knowledge you need to develop in order to ensure your future success and employability?

✓ What opportunities for learning should you be looking for both inside and outside your present job?

Use the Skill-Building checklist on page 121 to identify skills you want to develop.

4. Keep Growing Your Network.

You probably learned about networking when you were looking for work; in fact, maybe it was through your network that you landed this job! But just because you are employed doesn't mean you should stop networking. It is important to continue to nurture a wide range of relationships and to add to your network so that you will have more opportunities when you are ready to make a career transition. With this in mind, consider the following questions:

✓ Do you meet with and relate to a lot of different kinds of people who live and work in a variety of places or do you need to expand your network?

"Your future depends on many things, but mostly on you."

- Frank Tyger

"When I look into the future, it's so bright it burns my eyes."

- Oprah Winfrey

✓ Do you stay in touch with people for the sake of nurturing the relationship or do you call them just when you are looking for work?

✓ Who did you meet when you were looking for work that you would like to keep in touch with? (e.g., teachers, counselors, employers, fellow students or work seekers, etc.)

5. Make the Most of Your Current Work Situation.

Examine the work you are currently doing and ask yourself if it is providing experiences or new skills that enhance your livelihood. Seek out tasks or assignments that will grow and stretch you. Look for ways that you can add value to the employer. Think of everyone you work for as a *client* rather than a boss. Find ways to shine in the eyes of the customer! Use the 30 skills you learned in this guide to shine in everyone's eyes!

6. Find Mentors.

Obviously, directing your career in today's work world takes a combination of resourcefulness, creativity, and self-reliance. Few people have the luxury of time to juggle the pressures of their current jobs while looking out for their career paths – alone. And you don't have to do it alone. In fact, few successful people ever have. Hooking up with a mentor will help you apply some of these steps to career success.

7. Celebrate each step of the journey!

In your heart, keep a spot where you nourish your dreams. In your mind, keep a wide open sky where stars shine. Then, take a deep breath and relax. Don't worry about "big career decisions". Simply deal with the much smaller choices that you face day to day and you will find yourself *growing into options*. The important thing is to enjoy the place where you are at while you are there! Living only for the future is a waste of the present. We can only live 'happily ever after' moment by moment. Don't miss the treasure sitting at your feet by keeping your gaze in the future.

"I am not afraid of tomorrow, for I have seen yesterday and I love today."

- William Allen White

"It is better to look ahead and prepare than to look back and regret."

- Jackie Joyner-Kersee

Skill-Building Checklist

An important part of career development is taking responsibility for your own professional growth and skill building. Use this survey as a way of identifying key skill areas in which you would like to grow and develop.

(a) Place a check (✓) next to those skill areas that you think are important to success on your job.

(b) Place two checks (✓✓) next to each of the skill areas below in which you would like to improve.

(c) Circle those skill areas that you would like support or advice in devising a development plan or working with a mentor.

_____ Assertiveness   _____ Computer skills

_____ Decision-making   _____ Networking

_____ Listening   _____ Keyboarding skills

_____ Information gathering   _____ Managing time

_____ Team playing   _____ Goal-setting

_____ English as a second language   _____ Stress management

_____ Public speaking   _____ Writing

_____ Planning   _____ Learning

_____ Negotiating   _____ Customer service

_____ Supervising   _____ Working independently

_____ Using feedback   _____ Using office equipment

_____ Specific technical skills (specify below)

To The Reader

Thank you for taking this journey and congratulations for surviving the rocky road of being a new employee! May your on-going journey be filled with both work and play, innocence and wisdom, the thrill of new roads taken and the comfort of being at home in the world. Happy travels and keep your face to the sun!

Denise Bissonnette

"Afoot and light-hearted
I take to the open road
Healthy, free, the world before me,
The long, brown path
Leading wherever I choose."

- Walt Whitman

"*If* *one advances in the directions of his dreams,*
And endeavors to live the life which he has imagined,
He will meet with a success unexpected in common hours."

- Henry David Thoreau

"There is no try . . . there is only do."

- Yoda, Star Wars, George Lucas

"*Don't be afraid of the distance*
Between your dreams and the reality.
If you can dream it, you can make it so."

- Belva Davis

"*Depending on the circumstances*
You should be solid as a diamond;
Flexible as a willow;
Smooth flowing like water;
Or, empty as space.
The important thing is to pay attention
And read your circumstances."

- Morikei Ueshiba,
The founder of Aikido, Japanese martial art

"*The secret to discovery lies not in seeing new landscapes,*
But in having new eyes."

- Marcel Proust

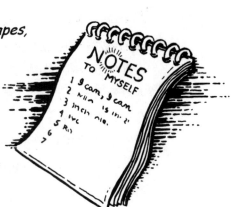

"*Do more than belong: participate.*
Do more than care: help.
Do more than believe: practice.
Do more than be fair: be kind.
Do more than forgive: forget.
Do more than dream: work."

- William Arthur Ward

"The human mind is a miracle.
Once it accepts a new idea or learns something new,
It never returns to its original dimensions.
It is limitless."

- Leo Buscaglia

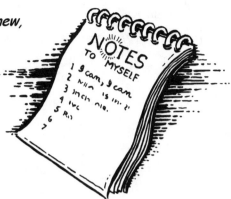

30 Ways to Shine

"*You can tell whether a person is clever by his answers. You can tell if a person is wise by his questions.*"

- Martin Luther King